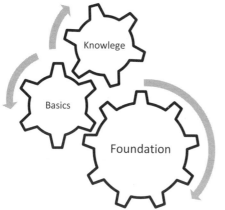

Teradata 12 Basics

An Authorized Teradata Certified Professional Program Study Guide

Exam TE0-121

First Edition

ISBN 978-0-9830242-0-0
Printed by Cerulium Corporation

Stephen Wilmes
Eric Rivard

Copyright

Trademarks

Special Acknowledgement

A special thank you to the following individuals that contributed to the Study Guide content: Marta Beckett, Susan Hahn, Julie Huber, Marianne Jew, and David Micheletto. And, to Lance Miller who helped bring the vision to reality.

About the Author - Steve Wilmes

Steve Wilmes founded Cerulium Corporation in 2007. As Chief Executive Officer, his goal is to establish Cerulium as a premier data warehousing Technology Company. Cerulium's strategic growth is globally focused on six lines of business including education, consulting, BI solutions, productivity tools, application integration and assessment services. These lines of business have been highly successful by utilizing strategic data warehousing solutions provided by Teradata that spans across the consumer, and commercial markets.

Mr. Wilmes has over 20 years of experience in the computer industry and is known to be a detail oriented, results-focused leader. He is an internationally recognized expert in several aspects of data warehousing including hardware, software, SQL, operating systems, implementation, data integration, database administration, and BI solutions.

Mr. Wilmes earned a bachelor's degree in business administration and economics in 1994 from Augsburg College and he is also a Teradata Certified Master.

Mr. Wilmes resides just outside of Columbia, South Carolina, with his wife, Becky. He has been involved with numerous civic, educational, and business organizations throughout his career. Some of his more recent associations include working with the Richland County Sheriff's Department – Region 4 Community Member, and volunteer for local organizations where he shares his technical expertise.

About the Author - Eric Rivard

Eric Rivard is the Vice President of Cerulium Corporation, and is responsible for consulting and product development operations. Mr. Rivard has substantial industry experience across the telecommunications, retail, and healthcare industries, and has consulted at many Fortune 500 companies. His in-depth knowledge of the Teradata platform has enabled him to design and develop customized Teradata applications. He has worked with some of the largest data warehouses in the world, providing unique software solutions and solving complex business problems.

Mr. Rivard dedicated the bulk of his career to the pursuit of data heterogeneity. Outside of this Teradata expertise, he worked extensively with a variety of database platforms, and developed software products that integrate across the different RDBMS platforms. He is an experienced Microsoft .NET developer, which has enabled him to use Microsoft's best-in-class development tools as a foundation for Cerulium Corporation's data warehouse applications.

Mr. Rivard resides just outside of Atlanta, Georgia, with his wife, Susana, and their three children. Outside of his professional career, he is actively involved in many community activities. In addition, he serves on the Advisory Board for the Management Information Systems (MIS) program at his alma mater, the Terry College of Business at the University of Georgia, where he earned his Bachelor of Business Administration in MIS and International Business.

Table of Contents

The Teradata Certified Professional Program

Enhance your knowledge and career

The Teradata Certified Professional Program (TCPP), launched in 1999, develops and manages Teradata's premier, and only, certification testing program. Teradata authorized training and proctored exams, available globally to customers, partners, and associates are instrumental in establishing an industry-standard measure of technical competence for IT professionals using Teradata technology. Recognized and valued by major global companies using Teradata, more than 51,000 Teradata Certifications have been awarded.

The new Teradata 12 Certification Track consists of seven exams that combine for achievement of six certifications and provides a logical progression for specific job roles. Starting with the core Teradata 12 Certified Professional credential, individuals have an opportunity to demonstrate knowledge by achieving Certification as a Technical Specialist, Database Administrator, Solutions Developer, Enterprise Architect, and the most prestigious Teradata Certification – Teradata 12 Certified Master.

The purpose of this Certification Exam Study Guide is to assist you in your goal of becoming Teradata Certified. The Guide will provide focused content areas, high level explanations around the key areas of focus, and help you to determine areas of further study prior to sitting for the Teradata Certification examination.

The Exam Study Guide will assist you in your Exam preparation, but you must be knowledgeable of the subject areas in order to pass the exam. This Guide is intended for individuals who have completed the recommended training and have the recommended amount of Teradata experience. We do not guarantee that you will pass the exam simply by reading the Exam Study Guide. Only hard work, hands-on experience, and a positive attitude will help you to achieve exam success. We wish you the very best of luck!

"The certification process promoted a systematic learning opportunity on a broad spectrum of topics. This enabled me to apply changes at work that never would have been done otherwise."
– Teradata Certified Master, Blue Cross Blue Shield of NC

The flowchart and matrix below are designed to help you define a path to the knowledge, skills, and experience needed to achieve Teradata 12 Certifications.

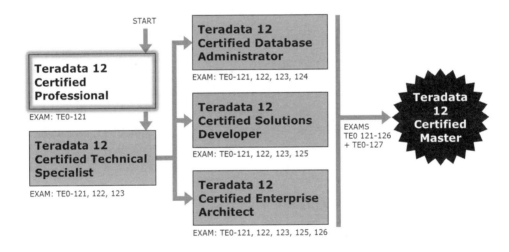

Teradata 12 Certifications		
Teradata 12 Certified Professional		
Exams Required:	Recommended Teradata Experience:	
• TE0-121 – Teradata 12 Basics	6-12 months	

Must be passed before continuing on certification path	Recommended Preparation Courses: • Introduction to the Teradata Database

Teradata 12 Certified Technical Specialist

Exams Required:

• TE0-121 – Teradata 12 Basics
• TE0-122 – Teradata 12 SQL
• TE0-123 – Teradata 12 Physical Design and Implementation

3 Exams to be passed in sequential order

Recommended Teradata Experience:

1-2 years

Recommended Preparation Courses:

• Introduction to the Teradata Database
• Teradata SQL
• Advanced Teradata SQL
• Physical Database Design
• Physical Database Tuning

Teradata 12 Certified Database Administrator

Exams Required:

• TE0-121 – Teradata 12 Basics
• TE0-122 – Teradata 12 SQL
• TE0-123 – Teradata 12 Physical Design and Implementation
• TE0-124 – Teradata 12 Database Administration

4 Exams to be passed in sequential order

Recommended Teradata Experience:

2-3 years

Recommended Preparation Courses:

• Introduction to the Teradata Database
• Teradata SQL
• Advanced Teradata SQL
• Physical Database Design
• Physical Database Tuning
• Teradata Application Utilities
• Teradata Warehouse Management
• Teradata Warehouse Administration

Teradata 12 Certified Solutions Developer

Exams Required:

- TE0-121 – Teradata 12 Basics
- TE0-122 – Teradata 12 SQL
- TE0-123 – Teradata 12 Physical Design and Implementation
- TE0-125 – Teradata 12 Solutions Development

4 Exams to be passed in sequential order

Recommended Teradata Experience:

2-3 years

Recommended Preparation Courses:

- Introduction to the Teradata Database
- Teradata SQL
- Advanced Teradata SQL
- Physical Database Design
- Physical Database Tuning
- Teradata Application Utilities
- Teradata Application Design and Development

Teradata 12 Certified Enterprise Architect

Exams Required:

- TE0-121 – Teradata 12 Basics
- TE0-122 – Teradata 12 SQL
- TE0-123 – Teradata 12 Physical Design and Implementation
- TE0-125 – Teradata 12 Solutions Development
- TE0-126 – Teradata 12 Enterprise Architecture

5 Exams to be passed in sequential order

Recommended Teradata Experience:

2-3 years

Recommended Preparation Courses:

- Introduction to the Teradata Database
- Teradata SQL
- Advanced Teradata SQL
- Physical Database Design
- Physical Database Tuning
- Teradata Application Utilities
- Teradata Warehouse Management
- Teradata Warehouse Administration
- Teradata Application Design and Development

Teradata 12 Certified Master*

Exams Required:

• TE0-121 - TE0-126: Successful completion of all exams and certifications **PLUS:**
• TE0-127 – Teradata 12 Comprehensive Mastery

7 Exams to be passed in sequential order

*Path for V2R5 Certified Masters (only)

• TE0-12Q: Teradata 12 Qualifying Exam for V2R5

PLUS:
• TE0-127 – Teradata 12 Comprehensive Mastery

Recommended Teradata Experience:

A minimum 5 years practical hands-on experience is highly recommended

Recommended Preparation Courses:

Taking all courses recommended for the Teradata 12 job role certifications:
• Introduction to the Teradata Database
• Teradata SQL
• Advanced Teradata SQL
• Physical Database Design
• Physical Database Tuning
• Teradata Application Utilities
• Teradata Warehouse Management
• Teradata Warehouse Administration
• Teradata Application Design and Development

Certification... Knowledge Building to Mastery

In today's economy, many companies are investing in the training and validation of employees' expertise and knowledge. Teradata's Certification process helps meet these discerning demands in the global market. Teradata has developed a new generation of certification exams and requirements that bring premium value to Teradata 12 Certification credentials.

Top 10 "What's new about the Teradata 12 Certification Track?"

1. Seven exams with all new content based on Teradata Database 12.0.
2. More rigorous certification criteria including a combination of training, study, and practical, hands-on experience.

3. Six new certifications require passing a combination of exams in sequential order starting with the Teradata 12 Basics exam.
4. Five Teradata 12 Certifications must first be achieved to gain eligibility for Teradata 12 Certified Master status.
5. A new Teradata 12 Comprehensive Mastery Exam, among other requirements, has been added to create a more rigorous Teradata 12 Master Certification track.
6. New IP security measures are in place to protect the integrity of exams and certifications.
7. Independent exam scoring procedure provides electronic Results Reports outside of the testing center.
8. Freshly designed certificates and logos available electronically.
9. New state of the art Certification Tracking System manages certification records, fulfillment, transcripts, and credentials validation.
10. The Teradata Certified Professional Program is well established with an experienced team available to support your successful Teradata Certification journey.

Path to Teradata 12 Mastery

A Teradata Certified Master enjoys a distinct advantage in the global marketplace. Employers seek Teradata Certified staff with verifiable knowledge and skills that support their business-critical Teradata systems. The TCPP Certification process helps those individuals who want to deepen their knowledge and build their skills to the highest level.

The path to achieve Teradata 12 Certified Master status is summarized in the matrix below.

If You Are...	Exams Required for Teradata 12 Master Certification
Starting on the Teradata 12 Certification Track	• TE0-121 – TE0-127 All 7 Exams required
Certified V2R5 Master	• TE0-12Q: Teradata 12 Qualifying Exam for V2R5 Masters • TE0-127: Teradata 12 Comprehensive Mastery Exam Both Exams required

The six core Teradata V2R5 exams were retired on March 31, 2010. Teradata V2R5 Certifications will not expire. However, individual V2R5 exams completed in the V2R5 Certification Track are not transferable to the new Teradata 12 Certification Track.

Exam Registration

All Teradata Certification exams are administered and proctored by authorized Prometric Testing Centers. Schedule exams at any authorized Prometric Testing Center by phone or online. In the US and Canada, you may call 1-877-887-6868. A listing of Prometric telephone numbers, by country, is available at: www.prometric.com/Teradata. Some countries do not offer online registration.

Where to Find More Information

To achieve your certification goals, pursue only Teradata-recognized processes and approved courses of study as outlined on the official

Teradata Certified Professional Program web site: www.Teradata.com/Certification. Information on all authorized Teradata Certification levels, exams, curriculum maps and recommended training, is supplied by a convenient matrix and links located on the TCPP web site.

Teradata Corporation's official certification exams and credentials are developed, copyrighted, and managed solely by the Teradata Certified Professional Program (TCPP) team. There are no other Teradata authorized exams, certifications, or legitimate credentials in the IT industry. To achieve your training and certification goals, pursue only authorized processes and approved courses of study as outlined on the official TCPP Website.

Chapter 1: Teradata Product Overview

Certification Objectives

- ✓ Describe the features and benefits of the Teradata technology
- ✓ Describe the uniqueness of Teradata in Data Warehousing
- ✓ Identify the benefits of Teradata automatically managed storage vs. Database Administrator (DBA) manually managed distribution techniques
- ✓ Identify platforms on which the Teradata RDBMS runs (OS and hardware)

Before You Begin

You should be familiar with the following terms and concepts.

Terms	Key Concepts
Shared Nothing	Virtual processors dedicated to disks
Linear Scalability	Processing in parallel and data growth
Teradata Platforms	Hardware systems supported

The Teradata RDBMS

Teradata is a Relational Database Management System (RDBMS), manufactured by Teradata Corporation, and is designed to support databases ranging from less than one terabyte to thousands of terabytes. This makes Teradata an obvious choice for both mid-range and very large data warehousing applications. Teradata enables its customers to answer virtually any question about its business, and to provide them with the answers they need to compete in today's marketplace.

With its parallelism and scalability, Teradata allows you to start small and grow very large, through linear scalability. Teradata is an open system; it is compliant with industry ANSI standards. Teradata can be accessed using SQL (Structured Query Language), which is used as the basis for ad hoc requests, as well as Business Intelligence (BI) tool integration.

Unlike traditional Online Transaction Processing (OLTP) databases, which are designed for the rapid processing of small amounts of transactional data, Teradata is designed to be a data warehouse system. Data warehouse systems are designed to process large amounts of data, very quickly and efficiently.

Teradata's Unique Features

Single Data Store

Teradata's ability to store large amounts of data gives it the ability to store all of the organization's data, in a single repository. Unlike other RDBMS systems, where data is often fragmented and replicated across multiple data stores, the Teradata Database is built to accommodate the data for the entire enterprise.

Having a single data store eliminates the space overhead associated with multiple data stores, along with guaranteeing a single, centralized copy of the data. The potential for data discrepancies is minimized and database administrators are not burdened with the movement of data across disparate sources.

Multiple applications can concurrently connect to Teradata and query the database. With all the data in a single data store, an application can communicate with virtually all facets of the business.

Shared Nothing Architecture

Teradata is a Shared Nothing Architecture. Each Teradata node, and their AMPs, operates independently from the rest of the nodes. An AMP, which is discussed further in Chapter 4, is referred to as an Access Module Processor (AMP). An AMP is responsible for data access. The AMPs each have their own disk space, which is not shared amongst the other AMPs, nor do AMPs connect directly to other AMPs.

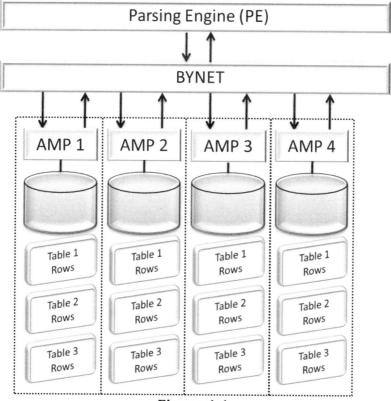

Figure 1.1

As illustrated in Figure 1.1, each AMP should have a relatively equal amount of rows from each table. Each AMP has a direct connection to the network via the BYNET. AMPs do not rely on each other to complete their individual assignments nor do they inhibit each other's operations.

Parallelism

The Teradata Database's high performance is directly attributable to its parallel design, and is referred to as having "unconditional parallelism". No special data models, column range constraints, or data quantities are required to make Teradata parallel; it is parallel by design. The Teradata Database is comprised of many separate virtual processors, all working in tandem, to answer a user's question.

Unlike OLTP systems, which are typically Symmetric Multi-Processing (SMP) based, Teradata is a Massively Parallel Processing (MPP) system. An MPP system outperforms SMP systems when processing large amounts of data, because an MPP system divides its workload evenly across its entire system, whereas an SMP system does not. Just as dividing up assignments across multiple employees allows more work to get accomplished in a short amount of time, Teradata splits up its assignments amongst its worker processes, allowing for more queries and larger amounts of data to be processed in a shorter period of time.

Linear Scalability

Linear scalability ensures that Teradata is highly scalable (currently up to 1024 nodes). Linear scalability dictates that performance will improve, and not diminish, as the system grows. The addition of AMPs will proportionately increase a system's performance capabilities. Basically, you can double the performance of a Teradata system by doubling the number of AMPs and their supporting nodes. Figure 1.2 depicts the doubling of AMPs on our sample Teradata system.

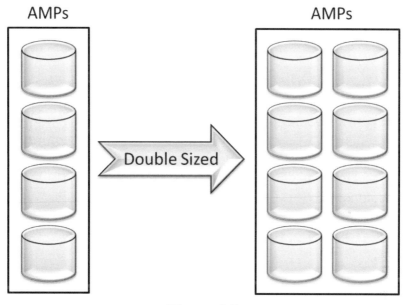

Figure 1.2

Scalability translates into flexibility and affordability. A scalable system means that it can start small and grow according to the needs of the business, without the threat of system degradation, as the system grows in size.

Mature Optimizer

The Teradata Database Optimizer (discussed in further detail -- Chapter 4) has been refined and enhanced throughout Teradata's history. While the basic concepts of the Teradata Database have changed little since its inception, Teradata has continued to innovate and re-architect its Optimizer. With each new version of the Teradata RDBMS, the Optimizer has become more mature and robust.

Unlike other data warehouse platforms, the Teradata Database Optimizer has the ability to perform multiple complex queries, multiple joins within a query, and virtually unlimited ad hoc processing. In addition, because the Optimizer is built in accordance with the Teradata Database's parallelism, it develops least-cost query plans that are both efficient and parallel.

Automatic Data Distribution

The Teradata Database automatically manages the distribution of data on its database. Other data warehouse platforms require manual intervention by the DBAs to efficiently distribute the data, in order to improve performance. Teradata handles the distribution, without requiring manual effort or distribution strategies.

Supported Platforms

The Teradata Database is supported on multiple operating systems, including Novel SUSE Linux (64-bit), Microsoft Windows Server (32-bit on older systems, 64-bit on newer systems), and UNIX MP-RAS (32-bit). UNIX MP-RAS is supported, but is being phased out in newer releases. Companies usually choose the OS that best fits their organizational design and needs.

The Purpose-Built Family Platform

Teradata offers a variety of platforms that are designed to meet specific analytical needs. Each platform utilizes the Teradata Database, giving customers a heterogeneous platform that allows for the reuse of data models, ETL, and underlying structures. Whether it is an active data warehouse, enterprise data warehouse, entry-level data warehouse, special purpose data mart, or a test and development environment, there is a platform that supports each business requirement.

Teradata Extreme Data Appliance 1550

The Teradata Extreme Data Appliance 1550 is designed for the processing of massive data volume and for strategic analytics. It is highly scalable, and is based on the processing design of the Teradata Active Data Warehouse 5550 platform. This platform is intended for a smaller number of users, who are typically working outside of the Enterprise Data Warehouse (EDW), to accomplish a specific business objective.

Teradata Data Mart Appliance 2500/2550/2555

The Teradata Data Mart Appliance 2500/2550/2555 is designed for very fast data access and deep-dive analytics. This platform is pre-configured and ready to run, allowing customers to rapidly implement the appliance into their environment. The Teradata Data Mart Appliance includes a powerful set of Teradata's Tools and Utilities, which enable customers to easily migrate to the EDW.

Teradata Active Enterprise Data Warehouse 5500H and 5555 C/H

The Teradata Active Enterprise Data Warehouse platform is designed for active data warehousing. This platform is designed and optimized for strategic and operational mixed workloads, high performance, power, and scalability. This platform is designed for full-scale EDW implementations and provides for the highest concurrency of users and applications.

Practice Questions

1) Which three Operating Systems are supported by Teradata?
    A. Windows 2003 Server
    B. SUSE Linux
    C. MVS
    D. UNIX MP-RAS

2) What are three of the features that make Teradata unique?
    A. Linear Scalability
    B. ANSI SQL
    C. Parallelism
    D. Single Data Store

3) Which three are parts of the Teradata Purpose-Built Family?
    A. Teradata Data Mart Appliance 2550
    B. Teradata Active Intelligence Data Warehouse 5550
    C. Teradata Active Enterprise Data Warehouse 5550
    D. Teradata Extreme Data Appliance 1550
    E. Teradata Extreme Data Mart Appliance 1150

4) In a Shared Nothing Architecture _____(choose two)
    A. Each AMP works independently from the other AMPs
    B. No AMP shares its hardware with another AMP
    C. Each AMP is dependent on other AMPs
    D. AMP's shares memory with other AMPs

5) Which two are benefits of Teradata's support for ANSI Standard SQL (choose two)?
   A. Submit queries from other database systems
   B. Can interface with BI tools
   C. Data is distributed automatically
   D. Queries get optimized to better plans

Chapter Notes

Utilize this space for notes, key points to remember, diagrams, areas of further study, etc.

Chapter 2: Data Warehouse Architectures

Certification Objectives

- ✓ Describe the layers of the physical Enterprise Data Warehouse (EDW) architecture
- ✓ Identify the components of the Data Warehouse architecture
- ✓ Identify Active Data Warehouse characteristics
- ✓ Describe the evolution of analytical processing and Active Data Warehousing
- ✓ Describe the basic concepts of Active Enterprise Intelligence
- ✓ Contrast centrally located architectures to physically distributed architectures
- ✓ Determine the benefits of centralized data warehouses vs. non-centralized data warehouses
- ✓ Describe the approach of building an Application Data Model vs. Enterprise Data Model
- ✓ Describe the characteristics of row vs. set processing
- ✓ Describe the characteristics of response time vs. throughput

Before You Begin

You should be familiar with the following terms and concepts.

Terms	Key Concepts
Data Layers	Staging, physical, and semantic layers
Active Data Warehousing	Evolution of data warehousing
Data Processing Options	OLTP, DSS, OLAP, and Data Mining
Data Processing Types	Row and Set Processing

Data Layers

The data in an EDW is managed, manipulated, and queried, in a variety of ways. Depending on the intended function, the method of handling data will vary. The data warehouse is considered to have three distinct data layers, which are classified by the mechanisms used to access and process the data as illustrated in Figure 2.1.

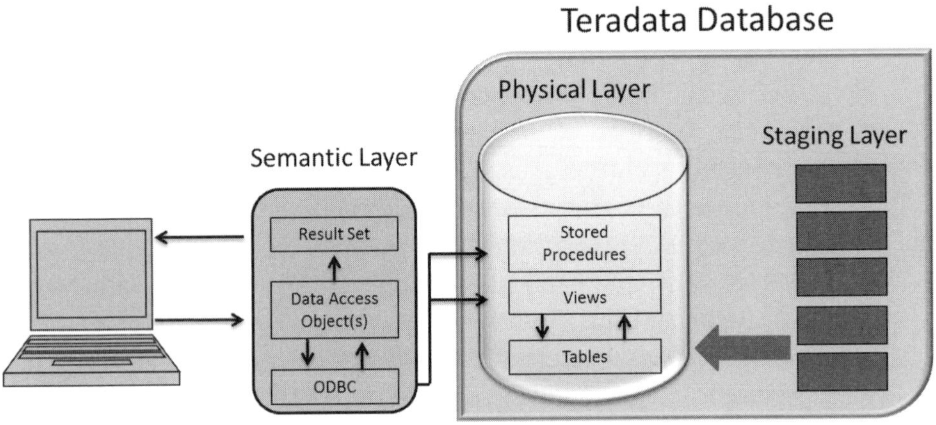

Figure 2.1

Staging Layer

The staging layer is the data extraction, load, and transformation area. Whether an ETL or ELT process is utilized, this is the layer where data is physically inserted into the data warehouse, in preparation for its full integration into the main tables in the database.

Physical Layer

The physical layer is where the data is structured for flexible, efficient, and business-friendly access. Denormalizations such as summary tables and pre-aggregations are built to provide the user with query flexibility and efficiency. In addition, Join Indexes (discussed in further detail -- Chapter 5) are also utilized to improve query performance.

Semantic Layer

The semantic layer is the business representation of the data. It is defined using business terms and is considered to be the access layer. Business Intelligence (BI) tools, cubes, and views are used to access this layer.

Active Data Warehousing

Evolution

As a data warehouse grows, and as it is further integrated into the day-to-day operations of the business, the ways in which the data warehouse is used begins to change. At first, data warehouses often solve a reporting need. Once fully implemented, the data warehouse can be used to achieve Active Enterprise Intelligence. Data warehouse usage typically evolves through five different stages beginning with Reporting, to Analyzing, to Predicting, to Operationalizing, and finally, to Active Data Warehousing.

Stages of Data Warehouse Evolution

Stage 1 – Reporting
Initially, data warehouses are most often used for historical reporting, such as monthly/quarterly/annual reporting. Reports are pre-defined, and used to provide basic information and analysis.

Stage 2 – Analyzing
Once reporting has been established, attention turns towards analyzing the results. At this stage, one tries to determine why the

actions occurred as well as begin to discover patterns in the data. Ad hoc queries and detail data analysis becomes more prevalent as you try to decipher additional meaning from the data.

Stage 3 – Predicting

After thorough analysis of the data has occurred, and once you have tremendous insight into what has occurred, the data warehouse is then used to predict what will happen in the future. Data mining tools and predictive models use historical data to forecast future results.

Stage 4 – Operationalizing

The data warehouse is moving from a strategic decision engine, into a tactical decisioning operation. Knowledge from the prior stages, which is typically available only to those working in a strategic role in the organization, becomes readily available to people in the organization that are making day-to-day decisions.

Stage 5 – Active Data Warehousing

Once the data warehouse has been operationalized, it migrates toward full automation, and becomes deeply integrated into most aspects of the enterprise's real-time operations. This stage is known as Active Data Warehousing. The data warehouse becomes involved in real time decisioning, such as displaying personalized offers to a customer on a web site, or performing complex customer operations, such as airline reservations.

Active Enterprise Intelligence

Active Enterprise Intelligence (AEI) is achieved once the Active Data Warehouse is fully integrated into the customer's business and technical architecture, providing 24/7 availability. As a result the Teradata Database is sufficiently able to handle large volumes of data, mixed workloads (strategic and tactical), concurrent users and applications, and the responsiveness needed to provide virtually minute-to-minute information.

Breaking down each word in AEI, it is "active" in that it has the capability to drive intelligent decisioning, very efficiently and on-demand. It supports the "enterprise" by providing a single view of the whole business, to both users and applications, across the business. Finally, the "intelligence" is derived from its ability to support both tactical and strategic decisioning, by aligning all of the enterprise's systems and business processes. The Teradata Active Data Warehouse (ADW) is all of Teradata's products, services, features, and business partnerships, combined together, in order to support the Active Enterprise Intelligence business strategy.

Evolution of Data Processing

In the past, data processing was separated into two distinct segments, Online Transaction Processing (OLTP) and Decision Support Systems (DSS). Today, data processing can be broken into four distinct segments, OLTP, DSS, OLAP, and Data Mining.

Online Transaction Processing (OLTP)

Online Transaction Processing systems are designed to support a large volume and high frequency of user requests in real time. However, these requests typically require a small set of rows and limited data processing. Typically, OLTP systems are purely transactional systems, such as web sites and ATMs.

Decision Support Systems (DSS)

Decision Support Systems are designed to process much larger data volumes than OLTP systems, and to perform data analysis, as opposed to real time transactions. DSS receives fewer requests than OLTP, but the requests are typically much more complex, and involve many rows and tables. A DSS is used to analyze detail data to look for historical trends, detect patterns, and make future predictions.

Online Analytical Processing (OLAP)

OLAP is a type of analytical processing found within a Decision Support System. OLAP data cubes allow for the "slicing and dicing" of facts along dimensions. This provides the user with greater insight into the data, greater flexibility in the amount of questions that can be asked and even quicker answers to complex business questions. A variety of generic OLAP tools are available, which facilitate the creation of the cubes and the reporting of the results.

Data Mining

In Data Mining, deep analysis of historical data is performed in order to discover patterns. These patterns are then used to create predictive models, which are used to determine future actions. Data Mining is very useful for forecasting purposes, such as customer purchase and inventory forecasting, churn analysis, and fraud detection.

Data Mining has two distinct phases. In the first phase, an analytic model is built, based on historical detail data. In the second phase, the model is applied to current data, in order to predict what may occur in the future (based on the past events found in the historical data).

Distributed Architecture

A true Enterprise Data Warehouse is a single platform with a centralized architecture, with all hardware and software components fully integrated. However, a physically distributed architecture describes a system where the data warehouse itself is distributed across multiple hardware and software components.

Depending on its usage, a data warehouse might fit either architecture. For example, a data warehouse that contains all of the enterprise data would be considered a centralized architecture. If a data warehouse only contains a portion of the enterprise data for a specific application purpose (i.e., Customer Relationship Management), it would be considered physically distributed in that it is separate from the EDW.

Centralized Data Warehouse

The purpose of a data warehouse is to act as a single centralized data store for the entire enterprise. Data from all operational systems are extracted and loaded into the data warehouse to provide a holistic view of the entire organization.

The centralized data warehouse eliminates the need for multiple, non-centralized data warehouses. Having a single, centralized data warehouse allows for cross-business analysis against accurate and timely data. Non-centralized data warehouses often contain inconsistent data and offer limited answers to complex business questions.

Figure 2.2 illustrates a non-centralized data warehouse. In this scenario, an end-user must query each source system, individually. Because each system is isolated from one another, cross-business questions are difficult to answer. For example, imagine a question such as "do customers call more often when the inventory is depleted for a popular product". This question is not easy to answer because the data resides in separate locations and cannot be queried on the same system.

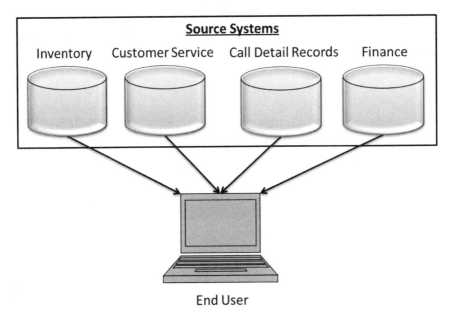

End User

Figure 2.2

Figure 2.3 illustrates the centralized data warehouse. The end user is able to query the Teradata Data Warehouse as a single data source as opposed to each individual system. In addition, the end user has the ability to join the different source systems together in their queries to answer cross-business questions.

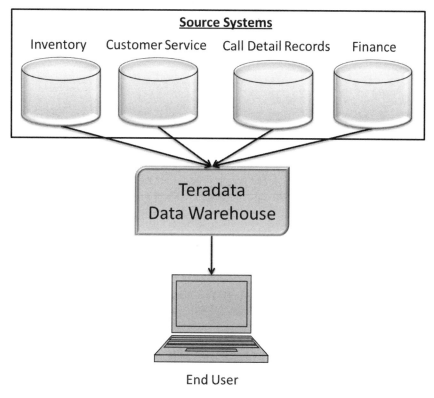

Figure 2.3

Data Marts

A data mart is a subset of data that is used to support a specific function or application. A data mart may contain both detail and summary data, but this data is often structured specifically (aggregated or filtered) for its intended application. There are three types of data marts: Independent, Logical, and Dependent. Figure 2.4 depicts how the different types of data marts might interact with a Teradata system.

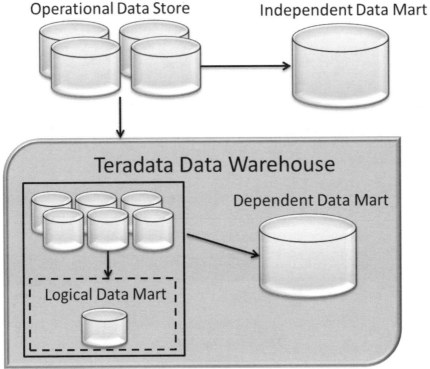

Figure 2.4

Independent Data Marts

Independent data marts are subsets of data that are sourced from one or more operational systems. The data is in a separate physical location from the originating data. Data is typically summarized and aggregated, and used for specific business applications.

Although independent data marts are easy to build, and may support smaller business requirements, they are costly to support. Data must be moved between sources, additional storage costs are required, and the data must be synchronized consistently and accurately. In addition, because the detail data does not exist on the independent data mart, only a limited number of questions can be asked of the data.

Logical Data Marts

Logical data marts are located in the same physical location as the rest of the data warehouse. Because an EDW stores all of the data for the business, it is relatively easy to create a virtual, or logical, data mart within the same data warehouse system. This enables the data mart to access all detail data from the rest of the data warehouse and minimizes data extraction, loads, and transformations.

A drawback to logical data marts is that they rely on the use of the detail data in the data warehouse, which is not aggregated or dimensionalized. However, Teradata's parallelism, and its ability to act as a single data store enables logical data marts to co-exist with the rest of the data warehouse, without severely impacting performance.

Dependent Data Marts

A dependent data mart is a subset of data that is created directly from the detail data in the data warehouse. Like an independent data mart, it requires the loading and transformation of data, and creates a separate repository of data. However, like the logical data mart the data may also reside on the EDW as well as a separate platform (i.e., a Teradata Appliance). Dependent data marts provide more flexibility than independent data marts, and have all of the advantages of the logical data mart.

Processing Types and Characteristics

Enterprise and Application Data Models

An Enterprise Data Model is used to map the entire enterprise. All aspects of the business, rather than a specific group, are included, in order to represent the entire organization. An Application Data Model is specific to a particular application, functional group, or area of the business.

In an Enterprise Data Warehouse, an Enterprise Data Model should be leveraged, as opposed to an Application Data Model, because the Enterprise Data Model encompasses all aspects of the business. An Enterprise Data Model provides the data warehouse with the flexibility to answer all questions across the organization, without regard to any specific business application.

Row and Set Processing

Depending on its design, a database can utilize one of two methods to process rows of data: row-by-row or set processing. Regardless of the chosen method, the rows are updated with a single command. However, each method has its distinctive qualities.

Row-by-Row Processing

In row-by-row processing, a single row is retrieved, and then the processing operation is performed, such as an update, insert, or delete. After that row has been processed, each subsequent row is completed and processed (one at-a-time) until all rows have been processed. Row-by-row does have an advantage over set processing, in that only one row is locked at-a-time, causing less lock contention (more than one user trying to access the same row, simultaneously) to occur.

Set Processing

In set processing, a set of relational data rows can be processed at once, without the need to process one at-a-time. This is significantly faster than row-by-row, in that 10 to 30 times the amount of data can be updated, at once. Set processing takes advantage of parallelism, and distributes the processing across all of the AMPs, in order to complete the data operation. Set processing is much more advantageous than row-by-row processing, when updating large volumes of data.

Response Time and Throughput

Response time can be defined as the amount of time elapsed between the beginning and the termination of an event, such as a query on a system. It is ideal to have the shortest possible response time. A short response time guarantees that results can be quickly returned to the requestor, enabling a faster decision to be made, based upon the returned data.

Throughput is a measure of how many concurrent tasks or transactions can be completed, per unit time. In order for a system to operate efficiently, it must be able to work on multiple requests at the same time. Otherwise, bottlenecks will occur, resulting in degraded system performance.

Teradata systems are designed for both optimal response time and throughput performance. Multiple queries can be processed, simultaneously (throughput), and the results are returned in the shortest amount of time possible (response time). If response time and throughput begin to degrade on a Teradata system, you can improve the performance by adding nodes, enabling workload management, or by decreasing the number of concurrent system requests.

Practice Questions

1) Place the Stages of Data Warehouse Evolution, in order:
    A. Operationalizing
    B. Reporting
    C. Active Data Warehousing
    D. Predicting
    E. Analyzing

2) Which data layer describes how the data is structured and denormalizations occur?
    A. Physical Layer
    B. Access Layer
    C. Semantic Layer
    D. Data Layer

3) Which two of the following describes Set Processing?
    A. Each row is processed, one-at-a-time.
    B. Rows are processed all at once
    C. Efficiently processes large amounts of data
    D. Best suited when applying updates to small amounts of data

4) Which one of the following accurately describes Online Analytical Processing (OLAP)?
    A. Typically used with only small sets of data
    B. Data cubes are created based on dimension and fact data
    C. Data is used to create predictive models
    D. Support a high volume of user requests, in real-time

Chapter Notes

Utilize this space for notes, key points to remember, diagrams, areas of further study, etc.

Teradata 12 Certification Study Guide

Chapter 3: Relational Database Concepts

Certification Objectives

- ✓ Define the terms associated with relational concepts
- ✓ Describe the advantages of a relational database
- ✓ Describe the differences between star schema and normal form logical models

Before You Begin

You should be familiar with the following terms and concepts.

Terms	Key Concepts
Logical Data Modeling	Primary and Foreign Keys,
Normalization	Types and descriptions of forms
Dimensional Modeling	Fact / Dimension, and Star Schema

Logical Data Modeling

A Logical Data Model (LDM) is a logical representation of the entities (and their attributes), and their inter-relationships, within a RDBMS. The LDM helps to provide an illustrated version of the business requirements.

The LDM describes the data structure of each entity, along with sample data. The depicted entities model real world entities such as people, places and things. The LDM is designed irrespective of its usage or data volumes.

Primary key and foreign key attributes are designated to provide an understanding of the entity's unique identifier and its relationships. Establishing relationships helps to illustrate the "big picture" of the model by showing how the entities inter-relate.

Figure 3.1 demonstrates a small portion of an LDM:

Entity: EMPLOYEE

Column Name:	EMP	DEPT	LNAME	FNAME	SALARY
Notations:	PK	FK			
Sample Data:	258	99	Lawson	Judy	205000
	369	01	Gatsby	Walter	100000
	654	25	Valdez	Jorge	30000

Figure 3.1

Primary Keys

A primary key is the designated attribute (or attributes) in an entity whose unique values will be used to identify each row in the entity. Most often, the best candidate is one small attribute that most appropriately represents the data in the row. Occasionally, multiple attributes may be necessary to serve as a primary key, in order to guarantee uniqueness.

Figure 3.2 shows the Customer and Area entities. The Customer entity has CUST_ID as its primary key, and the Area entity has AREA as its primary key.

Entity: CUSTOMER

CUST_ID (PK)	AREA (FK)	LAST_NM	FIRST_NM
333	3	Roark	Oscar
369	4	Gatsby	Walter
665	2	Mendoza	Manny

Entity: AREA

AREA (PK)	AREA_NAME
1	North
2	South
3	East
4	West

Figure 3.2

Foreign Keys

A foreign key is one or more attributes in an entity that relates to a primary key in another entity. A foreign key cannot have a non-null value without a corresponding value in the primary key entity.

Primary Key Compared to Foreign Key

Although Primary and Foreign Keys are used in conjunction to relate data together, there are some key differences between the two:

Primary Key
- Must not be null
- No duplicate values allowed
- Only one primary key per entity

Foreign Key
- Foreign key must have a corresponding primary key
- An entity can have zero or more foreign keys
- Duplicate values are allowed
- Null values are allowed

Figure 3.3 shows the same Customer and Area entities as in the previous example. Notice that the AREA attribute also appears in the Customer entity and it is designated as a foreign key. The attribute points back to the AREA attribute in the Area entity, where it is the primary key.

Entity: CUSTOMER

CUST_ID (PK)	AREA (FK)	LAST_NM	FIRST_NM
333	3	Roark	Oscar
369	4	Gatsby	Walter
665	2	Mendoza	Manny

Entity: AREA

AREA (PK)	AREA_NAME
1	North
2	South
3	East
4	West

Figure 3.3

Normalization

Normalization describes a series of techniques that are used to design database tables. These techniques, incorporated into the data model, help reduce redundancy and avoid structural problems that lead to data anomalies. Normalization ensures that the database design is well-formed and that it is not redundant. A normalized model includes entities, attributes, and relationships.

Normalization is broken down into different degrees referred to as "forms". Each form of normalization encompasses the form(s) before it. Below is a brief description of the first three normal forms.

First Normal Form (1NF)

1NF ensures the table/entity is free of repeating groups. For example, the employee table would not contain phone numbers, because every employee probably has more than one number, which would lead to repeating groups of data (i.e. phone numbers).

Second Normal Form (2NF)

2NF ensures that all columns/attributes can relate to the entire primary key and not just part of the key. For example, the employee table does not need a combination of employee id and last name. Only employee id is relevant in the relation.

Third Normal Form (3NF)

3NF ensures that all columns relate only to the primary key, and not to any other column. For example, the employee sales table should only contain sales information, and not irrelevant information, such as employee birth date, which belongs in the employee table.

A good data warehouse is in 3NF, because it helps to avoid redundant data, saves disk space, and reduces unsynchronized data. Eliminating redundant data strengthens data integrity and requires fewer updates to keep the EDW data in synch.

Dimensional Modeling

Fact Tables

Fact tables contain numeric measurements (such as aggregates, averages, and summations) or other fact information. Examples are sales totals, unit totals, quantities, etc. Fact tables primarily store the most important and quantifiable data about a business process. The fact table is surrounded by dimension tables, which are used to analyze or "dimension" the data within the fact table.

Table: FACT_SALES

DATE_ID	PRODUCT_ID	STORE_ID	SALES_TOTAL	QUANTITY
23	69354	201	97244.78	233
32	54897	954	95564.45	1510
43	44577	400	78724.49	855

Figure 3.4

In Figure 3.4, we have a table named FACT_SALES. This is a fact table that contains information about product sales, at a given store, on a given day. The primary key is comprised of a date id, a product id, and a stored id. The FACT_SALES represents an intersection with the product, date, and store dimensions.

Dimension Tables

Dimension tables are used to describe the information in fact tables, and are composed of attributes that are used for grouping, constraining, and reporting fact table data. The data contains the properties and characteristics of the object (i.e., product). The data in dimension tables is deep and is useful for querying and reporting. Without dimension tables, the information in fact tables would have little business meaning to the end-user.

Table: DIM_PRODUCT

PRODUCT_ID	PRODUCT_NAME	PRODUCT_MANUF	PRODUCT_CATEGORY
69354	Handy Wrench	2341	11
54897	Big Drill	5644	11
44577	Power Screwdriver	3525	35

Figure 3.5

In Figure 3.5, we have a dimension table named "DIM_PRODUCT". This table contains information about individual products, such as the product id, the product name, the product manufacturer, and the product category. Queries against the DIM_PRODUCT table provide the user with detailed information about the actual product, versus a fact table, which would only indicate that a particular product had been sold.

Star Schema

The dimensional model, which is composed of the dimension and fact tables, is commonly referred to as a Star Schema (also known as the Star Join Schema). In a star schema model, a fact table is surrounded by its related dimension tables. The star schema model is designed to be flexible, and this allows for the addition of new facts and dimensions. Dimensions and facts can be modified without significant impact to the rest of the system. A Snowflake Schema is another type of star schema that is commonly used in dimensional modeling.

A benefit of star schema is easier querying, flexibility, and improved performance. Query performance improves because the tables are joined together directly, rather than through complicated, multi-table relationships. Because there are fewer columns in the fact tables, less information must be processed, resulting in better performance. Dimensions ensure that many different questions can be asked, using the same base information, without query optimizations having to be made for each question asked.

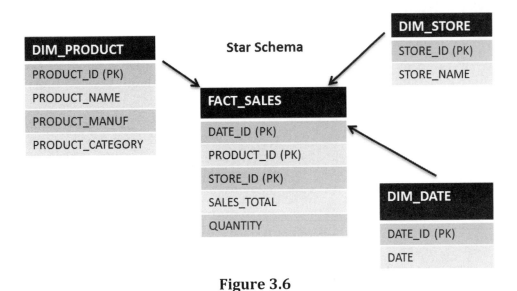

Figure 3.6

Figure 3.6 illustrates a sample star schema, made up of a single fact table, FACT_SALES, surrounded by product, store, and date dimension tables.

Practice Questions

1) Which two of the following are true about a Primary Key?
   A. A Primary Key must be unique
   B. One or more Primary Keys may exist on a table
   C. Null values are allowed
   D. No duplicate values are allowed

2) Which two of the following are true about a Foreign Key?
   A. A Foreign Key must be unique
   B. A Foreign Key must have a corresponding Primary Key
   C. Null values are allowed
   D. No duplicate values are allowed

3) Which statement is true when comparing the advantages of third normal form to star schema?
   A. Third normal form tends to have fewer entities
   B. Third normal form requires additional data storage
   C. Star schema requires additional data storage
   D. Star schema tends to have fewer entities

4) Which answer best describes First Normal Form (1NF)?
   A. All columns related to the entire primary key, not just part of the key
   B. Table is free of repeating values
   C. All columns relate to the primary key, and not to any other column
   D. All foreign key columns must not contain null values

5) Which answer best describes Second Normal Form (2NF)?
   A. All columns related to the entire primary key, not just part of the key
   B. Table is free of repeating values
   C. All columns relate to the primary key, and not to any other column
   D. All foreign key columns must not contain null values

6) Which answer best describes Third Normal Form (3NF)?
   A. All columns related to the entire primary key, not just part of the key
   B. Table is free of repeating values
   C. All columns relate to the primary key, and not to any other column
   D. All foreign key columns must not contain null values

Chapter Notes

Utilize this space for notes, key points to remember, diagrams, areas of further study, etc.

_____

_____

_____

_____

_____

_____

_____

_____

_____

_____

_____

_____

_____

_____

_____

_____

_____

_____

_____

_____

_____

_____

Chapter 4: Teradata RDBMS Components and Architecture

Certification Objectives

- ✓ Describe the components of the Teradata architecture
- ✓ Describe how internal Teradata components interact
- ✓ Define user defined space and use
- ✓ Identify the communication interfaces from external applications to Teradata
- ✓ Identify application interfaces

Before You Begin

You should be familiar with the following terms and concepts.

Terms	Key Concepts
PE	Parses, optimizes, and dispatches queries
BYNET	Communication layer
AMP	Accesses and manages the data
Database Space	Perm, Spool, and Temp
Connectivity	ODBC, JDBC, and CLI

Parsing Engine (PE)

The Parsing Engine's (PE) purpose is to formulate the most efficient and least expensive plan, in order to return the requested response set. The Parsing Engine consists of the Parser, the Optimizer, and the

Dispatcher. The plan is converted to executable steps, which are performed by the AMPs, and finally passed to the Dispatcher. The PE is also responsible for any necessary input conversions, such as a character set conversion from EBCDIC to ASCII.

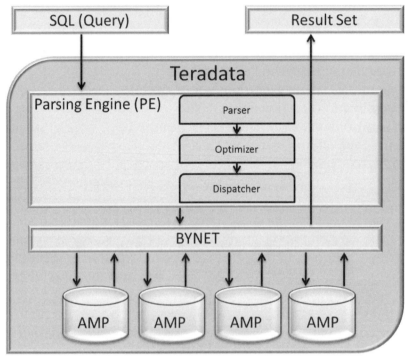

Figure 4.1

As illustrated in Figure 4.1, for every submitted request, the PE:

1. Verifies the syntax of the request (SQL)
2. Verifies the user's security permissions to determine if the target object (table, views, macros, etc.) can be accessed
3. Parses and optimizes SQL
4. Formulates the execution plan for the AMPs which includes breaking down the actual request into a series of steps
5. Returns result answer set back to the client

Teradata BYNET

The Parsing Engine does not communicate directly to the AMPs. Instead, a communication layer, known as the BYNET, sits between the AMPs and PEs. The PE transmits the plan to the AMPs via the BYNET. In response, the data that the AMPs retrieve from disks are returned to the PE via the BYNET. Each Teradata configuration has two BYNET channels (providing redundancy and additional bandwidth). The channels are bi-directional pathways that send and receive data concurrently, as illustrated in Figure 4.2.

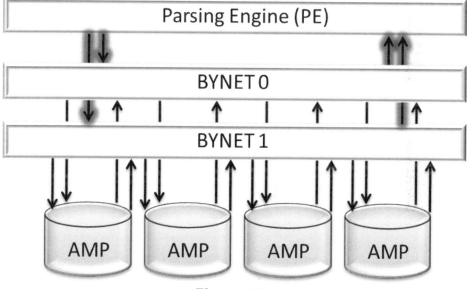

Figure 4.2

Access Module Processors (AMPs)

The Access Module Processors (AMPs) perform the physical task of retrieving the result data. AMPs also perform any necessary output conversions, such as data type conversions. The AMPs connect to a single virtual disk (VDISK), which is discussed further in Chapter 6.

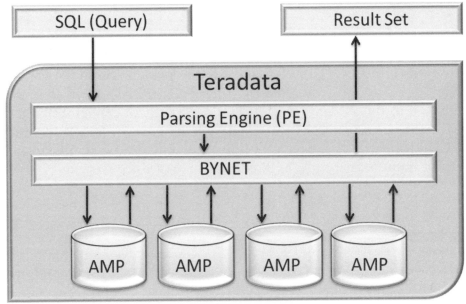

Figure 4.3

Figure 4.3 reveals how the AMPs operate. The rows of each table on a Teradata system are distributed evenly across all the AMPs and each AMP is responsible for the row retrieval for each table on their disk. The AMPs work independently and therefore retrieve data concurrently. Each AMP performs its portion of the work in parallel, which is a foundation of parallel processing. The AMPs are also responsible for aggregating columns, lock management, sorting rows, join processing, output formatting, disk space management, accounting, recovery processing, and special utility protocols.

Nodes

Teradata refers to each individual server within a system as a node, which is comprised of both hardware and software. Each node has its own operating system (OS), its own copy of the Teradata RDMBS software, CPUs, memory, and disk space.

In turn, a Teradata cabinet is comprised of one or more nodes, and a system can have more than one cabinet. Each node is connected to the BYNET, which is the communication path for the entire system.

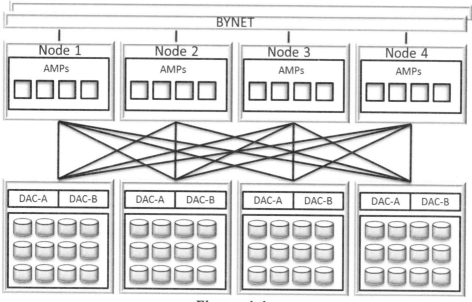

Figure 4.4

In Figure 4.4, we have a four node Teradata system. Each node has two Intel® processors and up to 32 GB of memory where the AMPs and PEs are configured. This is why AMPs and PEs are referred to as Virtual Processors (VPROCs). The node connects to both the BYNET and to a virtual disk set, which is a set of disks. The virtual disk is where the AMP's share of table data is physically stored.

Space Allocation

In Teradata, space allocation is defined as the amount of disk space that is permitted for a specific user or database. Space allocation acts as a ceiling, or upper-limit, not as a guaranteed amount. The amount of space a user or database can physically consume is based upon the actual space availability on the Teradata system.

Teradata has three different categories of space allocation: Permanent (Perm), Spool, and Temporary (Temp).

Permanent (Perm) Space

Permanent (Perm) space is the amount of data storage allowed for a specific user or database. This data storage includes the actual table data, secondary index sub-tables, fallback table data, and permanent journals. Perm space allocation is not a guarantee. If there is no more usable space available on any AMP for a specific user or database, a user or database cannot utilize its full definition.

With a new installation of Teradata, all Perm space in Teradata is owned by the system master account, DBC. The total amount of Perm space on the Teradata system would be the sum of all available Perm space, across all AMPs, divided by the number of AMPs. Available Perm space is always determined per AMP because Teradata distributes data as evenly as possible across all AMPs.

In Figure 4.5, we have a new Teradata system with 10 AMPs and 1 terabyte of total system disk space, which is currently owned by DBC. Divided by AMP, we have 100 GB of actual available disk space which defines the per AMP limit.

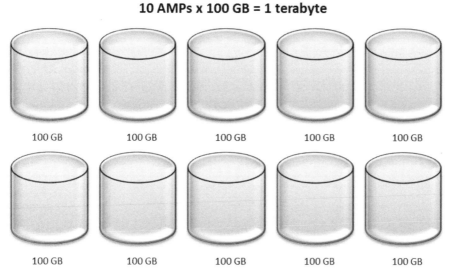

10 AMPs x 100 GB = 1 terabyte

100 GB	100 GB	100 GB	100 GB	100 GB
100 GB	100 GB	100 GB	100 GB	100 GB

Figure 4.5

Perm Space Limits and Hierarchy

User accounts and databases exist in Teradata as part of a hierarchical structure. The DBC user is the master, and sits on top of the entire Teradata hierarchy. When a new user or database is added to the system, a parent user must be designated. Once created, a user can have its own child users and/or databases, which can, in turn, have their own child users and/or databases.

In Teradata, space allocation is driven by the hierarchy. When a new database (or user) is created, it will need to have space available for the creation of tables and other objects. The amount of allocated space is zero at creation; there is no default value that may be specified. The parent database (or user) must give the new database some of its own allocated space. However, the amount of space allocated to a child database or user can remain zero.

Once space is allocated to the new database, the space available to the parent is lessened. However, if the child database is dropped, the space allocation is once again available to the parent. Likewise, when table data is deleted, or when a table (or other object) is dropped, the space is returned to the parent database/user.

Combined total = 1 terabyte

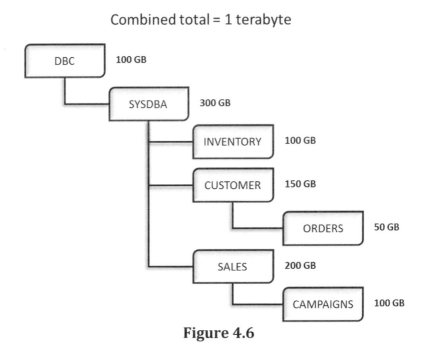

Figure 4.6

Figure 4.6 illustrates a 1 terabyte Teradata system in which DBC has dispensed 600 GB of its Perm space to the Sales, Inventory, and Customer databases. The Sales database, which originally had 300 GB of allocated space, has given 100 GB of space to its child database, Campaigns. The Customer database has given 50 GB of its space to Orders. If the Campaigns or Orders database is dropped, their space will be return to their respective parent.

Spool Space

Spool space is the disk space that is used to store a submitted query's intermediate and final result sets. All users who query Teradata must have Spool space allocated. The defined Spool amount for a user is a shared resource. As a user's Spool accumulates across all of their sessions, the Spool utilization may exceed the user's defined limit. When this occurs, the youngest request will abort, releasing its Spool to the other running sessions, and an error message is returned to the user. To minimize this occurrence, Teradata will automatically release Spool whenever it is no longer required for the processing of the request, or when the request has completed.

Spool space is allocated from the unused Perm space on a Teradata system. However, Spool space works differently from Perm space in that it can be allocated from any available space on the system (it does not require inheritance). Like Perm space, Spool space availability is limited to the amount available to the AMPs. Once the AMP runs out of Perm space, there will be no Spool available.

Figure 4.7 shows how Perm and Spool might exist on a 1 terabyte, 10 AMP, Teradata system:

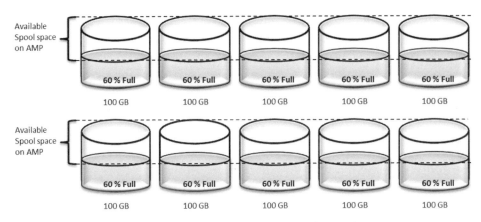

1 terabyte Teradata system

10 AMPs

40% of available Perm space is unused on each AMP.
A total of 400 GB is currently available for Spool.

Figure 4.7

Temporary (Temp) Space

Temporary (Temp) space is disk space that is available for use in Global Temporary Tables. A user can use Temp space to populate data into their pre-defined Global Temporary Tables. When the user logs off their session, the data is purged from the Global Temporary Table and its hold on the space is released.

Like Spool space, Temp space comes from the unused Perm space on a Teradata system. Temp space can also be allocated from any available space on the system, and does not involve inheritance. Like Perm and Spool space, a Temp space definition is divided by the number of AMPs to provide a per-AMP limit. Once the AMP runs out of Perm space, there will be no Temp space available.

Teradata Connectivity

Mainframe Connections

Hardware

To connect to Teradata from a mainframe, a physical connection is required. A mainframe can either connect directly using an ESCON connection or using BUS/TAG cables, and then to a Host Channel Adapter. The Host Channel Adapter connects to a dedicated Parsing Engine (PE).

Software

The mainframe connects (via utilities, such as BTEQ, or other applications) to the CLIv2 and the Teradata Director Program (TDP). The CLIv2 issues commands directly to Teradata, and is responsible for request and response control, parcel creation and blocking/unblocking, buffer allocation and initialization. The TDP provides Teradata with information about the client so that it knows how to properly format the result set for the client and it handles session balancing and failure notification.

Channel Attached Configuration

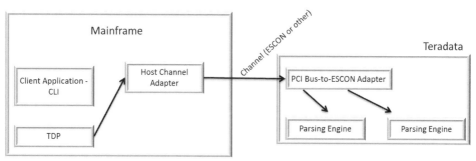

Figure 4.8

Local Area Network Connections

To make a successful connection between Teradata and a PC on the Local Area Network (LAN), both hardware and software components are required.

Hardware

An Ethernet network interface card is required to allow a computer to connect to the network, on both the Teradata system and each client PC.

Client Software

The CLIv2 (Call Level Interface) issues commands directly to Teradata and handles blocking/unblocking requests. The MOSI (Micro Operating System Interface) is a library of routines that handles the operating system and the networking interface. The MTDP (Micro Teradata Director Program) is a library of session management routines, ported for the specific operating system, and is linked into applications running on the network host. Finally, ODBC, JDBC, and OLE DB drivers are used to communicate from the client computer to the MTDP.

Teradata Software

The Gateway controls access between the LAN computers and Teradata. The Gateway controls user logons and can enable or disable user access. On the Teradata node, the AMP, PE, and PDE (Parallel Database Extensions) software handle the data request and retrieval.

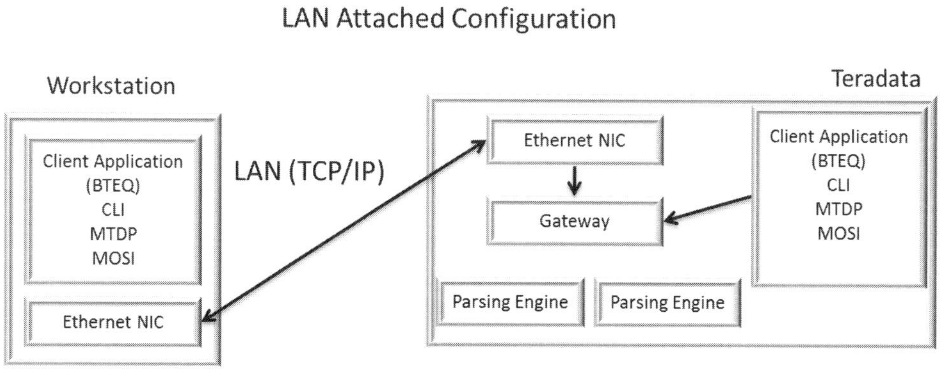

Figure 4.9

Application Programming Interfaces (APIs)

ODBC

The most common way to connect to Teradata is via ODBC (Open Database Connectivity). ODBC is a standard software API, supported by most operating systems. In addition, ODBC is supported by most RDBMS systems, making it one of the more popular connection methods. Most query tools, including Teradata's SQL Assistant, support ODBC.

OLE DB

Another popular method of connecting to Teradata is via OLE DB (Object Linking and Embedding). Created by Microsoft, OLE DB is a standard software API, supported by most operating systems and by most RDBMS systems. While some query tools support OLE DB, it is most often used by ETL, program code, and other software applications.

JDBC

When programming in a Java/J2EE environment, the recommended connectivity method is the Teradata JDBC (Java Database Connectivity) driver. The Teradata JDBC driver is fully managed code and is written in Java.

Call Level Interface (CLIv2)

The Teradata Call Level Interface (CLI), also known as CLIv2, is a collection of callable routines that speak natively to Teradata, and can be invoked by outside applications. Because the CLIv2 speaks directly to Teradata, it is an extremely efficient mode of communication. The CLI allows applications and users on both LAN and mainframe attached systems to communicate with Teradata directly, rather than using ODBC, OLE DB, or other protocols.

Practice Questions

1) Which two of the following are true about the Parsing Engine (PE)?
    A. Responsible for the communication between the AMPs
    B. Verifies the syntax of the SQL
    C. Physically retrieves data from the disk
    D. Returns the result answer set back to the client

2) Which three answers best describe how the PE, BYNET, and AMPs interoperate?
    A. The BYNET retrieves the data from the disks and returns the results back to the PE
    B. The PE transmits the query plan to the AMPs via the BYNET
    C. The AMPs receive the request from the BYNET and physically retrieve the data from the disks
    D. The AMPs pass its share of the data back to the BYNET

3) Choose the three types of space in a Teradata system.
    A. Temporary space
    B. Virtual space
    C. Permanent space
    D. Spool space
    E. Disk space

4) Which of the following types of space is utilized by Global Temporary Tables?
    A. Temporary space
    B. Virtual space
    C. Permanent space
    D. Spool space
    E. Disk space

5) Which of the following types of space is utilized by intermediate query results?
   A. Temporary space
   B. Virtual space
   C. Permanent space
   D. Spool space
   E. Disk space

6) Teradata SQL Assistant utilizes which of the following Application Programming Interface?
   A. ODBC
   B. OLE DB
   C. JDBC
   D. CLIv2

Chapter Notes

Utilize this space for notes, key points to remember, diagrams, areas of further study, etc.

Teradata 12 Certification Study Guide

Chapter 5: Database Managed Storage and Data Access

Certification Objectives

- ✓ Explain the purposes of the Primary Index
- ✓ Describe the differences between Primary Index and Primary Key
- ✓ State the reasons for defining a UPI (Unique Primary Index) vs. a NUPI (Non-Unique Primary Index)
- ✓ Describe the differences between non-partitioned, single level, and multi-level partitioned tables
- ✓ State the reasons for defining a PPI (Partitioned Primary Index) and/or Multi-level Partitioned Primary Index (MLPPI)
- ✓ State the reasons for defining a USI (Unique Secondary Index) vs. a NUSI (Non-Unique Secondary Index)
- ✓ Describe the benefits of Join Indexes
- ✓ Describe the trade-offs between Index access and Full Table Scans
- ✓ Describe the operation and/or causes of Full Table Scans
- ✓ List the types and levels of locking provided by Teradata

Before You Begin

You should be familiar with the following terms and concepts.

Terms	Key Concepts
Primary Indexes and Data Distribution	Understanding UPI, NUPI, PPI, and MLPPI
Secondary Indexes	Utilizing USI, and NUSI for query performance

Join Indexes	Single table, multi-table, and aggregate
Locking	Types and levels of locks

Data Distribution Management

Data distribution is managed automatically by the Teradata Database. The database administrators (DBAs) are not required to perform onerous data re-organizations. In addition, no complicated indexing schemes are needed to guarantee that the data is evenly distributed. Data is distributed automatically, based upon each table's specified Primary Index.

Primary Indexes

All tables must have at least one column specified as a Primary Index. The Primary Index is specified at table creation and can never be changed without dropping and recreating the entire table. A table may not have more than one Primary Index, but the index may consist of one or more columns, with a maximum of 64 columns.

The Primary Index is pivotal to Teradata tables, for the following reasons:

Data Distribution

The selection of the Primary Index columns directly determines the distribution of the table's rows. Ideally, the rows should be distributed as evenly as possible across the AMPs, so a Primary Index that guarantees good distribution should be carefully considered. If distribution is poor, the performance will suffer during full table scan operations because only a portion of Teradata's AMPs are busy processing data.

Data Retrieval

The Primary Index is the fastest way to retrieve data. Because all data is distributed according to the Primary Index, it will physically provide the quickest route to the data.

Join Performance

The Primary Index can significantly impact the performance of query joins.

Primary Index and Primary Key

A Primary Index is different from a primary key in that its values can be non-unique, its values can change, and its purpose is not for row identification, but rather for data distribution.

The Primary Index is often, but not necessarily the same column(s) as the primary key. This is because the Primary Index is designed to be the best physical path to the data, whereas the primary key is intended to be the best logical path to the data. The Primary Index, by design, maximizes performance and accessibility.

Unique Primary Index (UPI)

In a Unique Primary Index (UPI), all values in the Primary Index column(s) must be unique, with no duplicate values in any other row in the table. Any row inserted with a duplicate value in the Primary Index column will be rejected. Note, for multi-column Unique Primary Indexes, each individual column may be non-unique, but the data values in the column combination must always be unique.

The UPI will evenly distribute the rows across all the AMPs. Therefore, a UPI is usually the best type of Primary Index to select when creating a table. The UPI also ensures that data is retrieved on the fastest physical path because a UPI accesses the data as a one AMP operation, and no duplicate checking must be performed.

In Figure 5.1, you will see that the CUST_ID column has been selected as the Unique Primary Index.

Table: CUSTOMER, with UPI on CUST_ID

CUST_ID	AREA	LAST_NM	FIRST_NM
333	3	Roark	Oscar
369	4	Gatsby	Walter
665	2	Mendoza	Manny

Figure 5.1

Non-Unique Primary Index (NUPI)

In a Non-Unique Primary Index (NUPI) the values in the Primary Index column(s) are NOT required to be unique. A NUPI may consist of one or more columns. In a NUPI, duplicate values in other table rows are allowed. Because duplicate values are allowed and they may occur frequently, the NUPI will not evenly distribute the rows across all the AMPs. However, based on the number of duplicate values, the quality of the data distribution will vary (less duplicate values equal better data distribution).

Because of the data duplication and distribution, the NUPI is usually a less efficient type of Primary Index than the UPI. However, even though the NUPI is not evenly distributed, it can still be a very effective way to retrieve data and NUPIs are very efficient for query access and joins.

Teradata 12 Certification Study Guide

In Figure 5.2, you will see that the LAST_NM column has been selected as the Non-Unique Primary Index, and that duplicate values exist in the column.

Table: CUSTOMER, with NUPI on LAST_NM

CUST_ID	AREA	LAST_NM	FIRST_NM
333	3	Roark	Oscar
345	1	Roark	Carol
369	4	Gatsby	Walter
665	2	Mendoza	Manny

Figure 5.2

Partitioned Primary Index (PPI)

The Primary Index is designed to distribute the data evenly across the AMPs. However, the data may not be distributed in such a way that is conducive to user data requests. A table can be distributed across all the AMPs, with no regard to how that data should be logically ordered. On Primary Index columns that have range-based data, such as date values, Teradata is often forced to perform a Full Table Scan to retrieve all the dates within the SQL statement's specified range.

To solve this data management problem, Teradata has the Partitioned Primary Index (PPI), which specifies how the user wants the table data to be physically organized on the AMPs, within the Primary Index. The data will still be distributed across all AMPs, but the specified data ranges will be grouped together on each AMP. The partition is defined within the Primary Index declaration in the table's DDL statement.

There are several advantages of using a PPI versus a table without a PPI (which is referred to as a "non-partitioned table" or a "NPPI"). When a query is submitted, Teradata will have a much easier time locating the data, since the PPI is ordered with the data in mind, thus reducing the likelihood of a Full Table Scan. Using partition elimination, the Optimizer can avoid entire partitions of data that are not within the range of the partition column, within the requested answer set. Finally, PPIs allow for the rapid deletion and insertion of data. PPIs yield the biggest performance on large tables, but the SQL statement must always include the range constraint.

Multi-Level Partitioned Primary Index (MLPPI)

A Multi-Level Partitioned Primary Index (MLPPI) allows a partition to be sub-partitioned. A Single-Level PPI is only one-level deep; in that only a single range or case expression is partitioned. In a MLPPI, additional partition expressions can be specified, which provides the Optimizer with additional access paths to the data. The Optimizer utilizes the additional partition expressions to further pinpoint the targeted data, through enhanced partition elimination. A MLPPI must have at least two specified partitions.

For instance, a table that has a MLPPI on sales date and area code can help improve the performance on queries that commonly search for sales, during a specified timeframe, within different area codes. Using partition elimination, the Optimizer scans through only the data on the AMPs that fall within the date range, and within the specified area codes.

Secondary Indexes

Primary Indexes are the quickest path to data, but only a single Primary Index can exist on a table. However, there are often other, equally important, columns on a table which are repeatedly accessed (WHERE clauses). Because they are not specified as the Primary

Index columns, the Optimizer often will choose to perform a Full Table Scan to return the result set.

Defining a Secondary Index will help to address these scenarios. A Secondary Index is similar to a Primary Index, in that it provides a path to the data. It improves the performance of individual queries and decreases the overall burden on Teradata by avoiding Full Table Scans. A Secondary Index is very useful in situations where table joining, aggregations, value comparisons, complex conditions, and character matching are required.

However, the Secondary Index operates quite differently than the Primary Index. The Secondary Index does NOT determine how rows are distributed across the AMPs. The column values of the Secondary Index are stored in a sub-table, which is spread across all AMPs. In addition, Secondary Indexes require both disk space and maintenance. Unlike the Primary Index, the Secondary Index is optional, and it does not have to be implemented at table creation. Secondary Indexes can be added and dropped, as necessary.

Figure 5.3 provides a quick reference to how the Primary and Secondary Indexes compare:

Primary Index vs. Secondary Index

	Primary Index	Secondary Index
Required	Yes	No
Can be unique or non-unique	Yes	Yes
Used for row distribution	Yes	No
Create and drop dynamically	No	Yes
Improves access	Yes	Yes
Create using multiple data types	Yes	Yes
Requires separate physical structure	No	Yes (subtable)
Requires extra processing overhead	No	Yes

Figure 5.3

Similar to the Primary Index, the Secondary Index allows for two different types of indexes: the Unique Secondary Index (USI) and the Non-Unique Secondary Index (NUSI).

Unique Secondary Index (USI)

A Unique Secondary Index (USI) must only contain unique values. The USI is efficient because the uniqueness ensures that Teradata can easily identify whether the SQL requested value even exists, by checking the Optimizer to see if any AMP carries the requested value. A Unique Secondary Index is also excellent for enforcing a primary key's uniqueness constraint. The USI is a two AMP operation, which is a significant improvement over an all AMP, Full Table Scan.

Non-Unique Secondary Index (NUSI)

Non-Unique Secondary Indexes (NUSIs) are often created on columns that are commonly queried and have reoccurring, non-unique, column values. The NUSI is an all AMP operation because every AMP has a Secondary Index sub-table that points to its own base rows.

When an SQL statement is executed with a NUSI column in the WHERE clause, the Parsing Engine directs all AMPs to check their sub-tables for matching rows. Each AMP will respond back with its rows, or indicate that it has none to return. Although each AMP is accessed, this is still much faster than a Full Table Scan, because the sub-table point directly to the requested rows.

Join Index (JI)

A Join Index (JI) is comprised of simple or aggregated information, from one or more tables. Join Indexes can significantly improve performance by storing information that is commonly joined or aggregated by user queries. Join Indexes are physical and require permanent space. A Join Index is automatically updated whenever the base table is updated.

The Teradata Optimizer will evaluate its options and determine whether to retrieve data from the base data or the Join Index. A Join Index is beneficial because it can avoid the need to access the base table or to perform aggregate processing. If more than one table is used by the JI, costly table joins and redistributions can be avoided, as well.

Based on how the Join Index is structured, it can be classified as a Single Table Join Index, Multi-Table Join Index, or Aggregate Join Index.

Single Table Join Index (STJI)

An STJI is the simplest type of Join Index. It is comprised only of rows from a single table. It provides an alternate and more efficient access path for the Optimizer, rather than the Primary Index, when joining to another table. The STJI can accomplish the join by accessing the data directly, without the redistribution of data across the AMPs.

Multi-Table Join Index (MTJI)

An MTJI is a Join Index that consists of two or more tables. The MTJI contains the result data for matched join columns. The Optimizer can use the MTJI, rather than the actual table joins, to more quickly and effectively return the data.

Aggregate Join Index (AJI)

Like an MTJI, an AJI can also consist of one or more tables. However, an AJI is different from an SJI and MTJI in that some of the columns in the Join Index are actually aggregations of data, rather than just the base table data. By pre-aggregating the data, the AJI helps to avoid the repeated aggregation of commonly executed calculations. This can be an extremely cost effective method of increasing query performance. An AJI can be used for SUM, AVERAGE, and COUNT functions.

Index Columns and Statistics

Statistics can be collected at either the index or column level, and should be refreshed whenever the rows in the table significantly change. To ensure that the Optimizer has the best information possible, it is recommended that you always collect statistics on index columns. If statistics are not collected, or stale, the Optimizer may choose to perform a Full Table Scan, which may significantly decrease performance.

Data Distribution on the AMPs

The Primary Index ensures that data is distributed across each AMP on the Teradata system. Therefore, every AMP must also hold a portion of table's data. Figure 5.4 illustrates a sample 4 AMP Teradata system with three tables. The data for each table exists on each AMP with the data spread as evenly as possible.

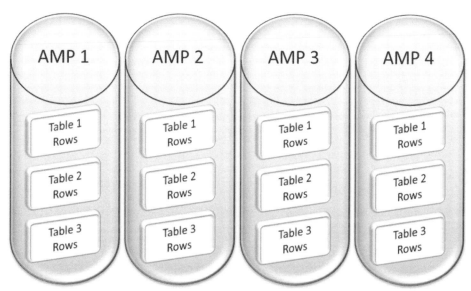

Figure 5.4

Unique Primary Indexes will always have good table distribution across all AMPs. This is because all the values are unique, and can therefore be distributed consistently without Teradata having to group duplicate hashed index values on the same AMP. In the following example, table Customer has a UPI of CUST_ID. Since each value in the Primary Index column must be unique, the data is evenly distributed across all AMPs, as seen in Figure 5.5.

AMP Distribution for Customer Table

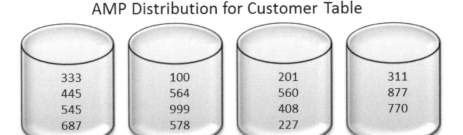

Figure 5.5

In Figure 5.6, table Shipping_Status has a NUPI on Shipping Status Code. Since only two values exist for shipping status ("yes" or "no"), you see that only two AMPs are actually used for storing this data. This will result in an uneven data distribution, and should be avoided. A Primary Index should only be chosen with columns that have a wide range of hashed values, in order to avoid data skewing on the AMPs.

AMP Distribution for Shipping_Status Table

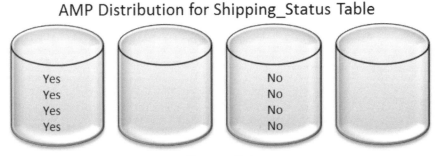

Figure 5.6

In Figure 5.7, table Customer_Payments, has a NUPI on payment date. Many different payment dates can occur, and the data is distributed (as evenly as possible) across all of the AMPs, according to their hashed values.

Teradata 12 Certification Study Guide

AMP Distribution for Customer_Payments Table

2009-01-05	2008-05-31	2008-11-12	2009-01-02
2009-01-05	2009-01-22	2008-06-01	2009-01-15
2008-11-21	2009-02-21	2008-07-25	2008-12-21
2008-05-06	2008-04-11	2008-05-03	

Figure 5.7

Access Methods

The Optimizer has its choice among different data access methods to retrieve the data on the AMPs. It evaluates each choice and selects the method which it determines to be the most efficient for the particular request.

Primary Index

Teradata always prefers to use the Primary Index to retrieve data. Because the Primary Index points directly to the AMP where the data is located, the Parsing Engine knows exactly where to go to get the data. This is the fastest method, but the Primary Index column(s) must be specified in the search criteria in order to leverage this access path.

Secondary Index

If a Secondary Index exists on the table, and if the Parsing Engine determines that the Primary Index cannot be used, then the Secondary Index will be used to retrieve the data. This is the second fastest method, but also requires that the Secondary Index column(s) appear within the query's search criteria.

Full Table Scan

When neither the Primary nor Secondary Indexes are specified as the access path, the Optimizer will request a Full Table Scan (FTS) to be performed against the entire table. When an FTS occurs, Teradata utilizes its parallelism capabilities to simultaneously retrieve the data from all of the AMPs. Because of parallelism, this may be the fastest method for accessing the data, if other access methods are determined to take longer than the FTS.

An FTS typically occurs when the user does not specify a Primary or Secondary Index column in their WHERE clause or if a Secondary Index is not strongly selective. However, it may also occur when a non-equality clause is used on an index column, or when a range of values is specified on an index column. In addition, if many duplicates occur within a non-unique index, the Optimizer may determine that an FTS is the most efficient way to sort through the data. Finally, the Optimizer may choose to perform an FTS if it determines that it is the most direct access path, which can occur if the table contains a very small number of rows.

The best way to avoid an FTS is to specify a value for each column in the Primary or Secondary Index, which increases the likelihood that the Optimizer will choose the index as its preferred access method. Ensuring that the Primary and Secondary Index columns are fairly unique also helps to ensure that the index columns will be chosen. The Primary Index determines data distribution but can also be useful in defining the best path to the data. However, because a Primary Index does not always translate into the best (or all conceivable) access paths, you can create Secondary Indexes that provide direct paths to the data. Finally, collecting index and column statistics, and refreshing the statistics as the data changes will also help to ensure that the Optimizer has the information it needs to determine the best access path.

Locking

Purpose of Locks

A lock is used to assert a type of privilege on an object in the Teradata Database, such as a database, table, view, or specific row(s) of data. Locks are used to guarantee data integrity during the execution of simultaneous and conflicting user requests. There are four different types of locks: exclusive, write, read, and access; each lock varies in its abilities and priorities.

Types of Locks

Exclusive

Exclusive locks are the most powerful and restrictive of all locks. They are applied at the database or table level (not the row level), and are automatically applied when performing a Data Definition Language (DDL) command, such as a CREATE or ALTER command. When an exclusive lock is applied, no other user request can access the locked database or table until the lock has been released. No other lock can be placed on the locked database or table, not even an access lock.

Write

Write locks help maintain data consistency while data is being updated. When a write lock is placed on the data, a user is not able to place any other type of lock on the data, except for an access lock.

Read

Read locks help to ensure that the data is not changed, guaranteeing data consistency, while the read operation is being performed. Exclusive and write locks cannot be placed on the data until the read lock has been released. However, an access lock can still be used.

Access

Access locks are used to allow a user to read data, even while the data is locked for read or write. Access locks are used when the user is not concerned with complete data accuracy. Access locks help to improve query response time, since the user is not forced to wait until other locks have been freed. When an access lock is used, an exclusive lock may not be granted to another user until the access lock has been released.

Locking Levels

Teradata supports different levels of locking, to ensure that the appropriate objects and rows of data are locked, based upon the requested lock.

Database

The lock is applied to all tables, views, macros and triggers within the database/user. This level of locking is the widest approach, locking the largest number of objects and data. This lock is useful when processing large amounts of data, across many objects.

Table/View

The lock is applied to all rows in the table, and to all tables referenced in a view. This lock is useful when working with large amounts of data, within a single table or set of tables.

Row

The lock is applied to one or more rows in a table, based upon the row hash. This lock helps to improve performance by minimizing the amount of data that is locked from other user requests.

Practice Questions

1) Which of the following three answers describe how a Primary Key differs from a Primary Index?
   A. Primary Key must be unique, a Primary Index does not need to be unique
   B. Primary Index must be unique, a Primary Key does not need to be unique
   C. More than one Primary Index can be defined on a table, only one Primary Key can be defined on a table
   D. Only one Primary Key can be defined on a table, only one Primary Index can be defined on a table
   E. Null values are allowed in a Primary Index, but not in a Primary Key
   F. Null values are allowed in a Primary Key, but not in a Primary Index

2) Which three of the following describe the purpose of the Primary Index?
   A. Data retrieval
   B. Data uniqueness
   C. Join performance
   D. Data distribution
   E. Enforces referential integrity

3) A PPI reduces the possibility of the Optimizer from electing to perform a Full Table Scan because (choose one):
   A. The Optimizer knows exactly which AMP the data physically resides upon
   B. The Optimizer checks each partition on every AMP for the requested data
   C. The Optimizer eliminates partitions of data not within the partition value range
   D. The Optimizer performs AMP sampling to determine the most likely location of the data

4) What three things are true regarding Primary and Secondary Indexes?
   A. More than one Secondary Index can exist on a table, as opposed to a single Primary Index
   B. Both are required on a table
   C. Primary Indexes improve data access whereas Secondary Indexes do not improve access
   D. Multiple columns can be used to define
   E. Can be unique or non-unique

5) What types of columns are good candidates for a Secondary Index (choose two)?
   A. Guarantee uniqueness
   B. Offer good data distribution
   C. Repeatedly accessed in WHERE clauses
   D. Commonly utilized in table joins

6) Which of the following is NOT a type of Join Index in Teradata?
   A. Single Table Join Index
   B. Aggregate Join Index
   C. Summary Table Join Index
   D. Multi-Table Join Index

7) Which of the following are true about Join Indexes (choose three):
   A. Can be directly selected by the user in a query
   B. Can be comprised of one or more tables
   C. May only consist of a single column
   D. Require Permanent space
   E. May contain simple or aggregated data

8) Which type of Index guarantees the best row distribution, across the AMPs?
   A. Unique Primary Index
   B. Unique Secondary Index
   C. Non-Unique Primary Index
   D. Non-Unique Secondary Index

9) Which one of the following objects cannot be locked in Teradata?
   A. Row
   B. Table
   C. Database
   D. Macro

Chapter Notes

Utilize this space for notes, key points to remember, diagrams, areas of further study, etc.

Chapter 6: Data Availability Features

Certification Objectives

- ✓ Describe how Transient Journals ensure data integrity
- ✓ Describe hardware specific data protection techniques
- ✓ Explain the concept of FALLBACK tables
- ✓ Describe the concept of node failover

Before You Begin

You should be familiar with the following terms and concepts.

Terms	Key Concepts
Transient Journal	Manages transactions and rollbacks
Fallback	Protects from AMP failures
Down AMP Journal	Supports data availability and recovery when an AMP fails
RAID 1, Cliques, and Hot Standby Nodes	Protects disk and nodes failures

Transient Journal

The primary responsibility of the Transient Journal is to keep a copy of the before images until either the transaction or rollback completes successfully. Once completed, the before images are deleted from the Transient Journal.

Figure 6.1 illustrates how the Transient Journal handles a row update. Remember, if the transaction is successful, the changes are committed. If the transaction fails, a rollback is performed, and the data is restored to its original state.

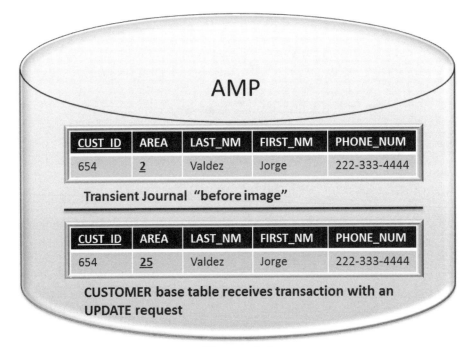

Figure 6.1

Specifically, the following occurs each time a SQL statement results in failure:

1) The submitting user receives an error message.
2) The transaction is rolled back and the data is returned to its original state.
3) Any locks are released.
4) All spool files associated with the request are released.

Note, the Transient Journal is an automatic Teradata process, and cannot be modified or disabled.

Fallback

Fallback is a data protection feature whose sole purpose is to avoid data loss during an AMP failure. If an AMP is lost due to a system failure, Fallback will ensure that a copy of the data exists on another AMP. Essentially, Fallback provides a duplicate copy of each row on the table.

The Fallback data is an exact copy and is updated concurrently from the primary data. Essentially, each data row has a twin image row on another AMP. Even though a mirror image can be said to exist, Fallback is not true data mirroring, because it spreads the duplicate rows across all of the AMPs. Fallback can be specified at either the table or database level.

Figure 6.2 illustrates a simple table on a 4 AMP system. If a single AMP fails, Teradata will automatically switch over to the Fallback data. In this example, if an additional AMP fails, Teradata will stop completely; since Fallback can no longer be assured. The following gives you a basic understanding of how Teradata organizes the rows across the AMPs.

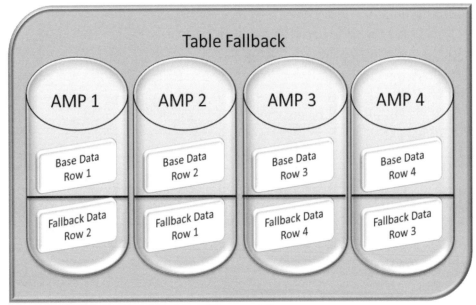

Figure 6.2

Fallback comes with a cost. Since the data is an exact copy, twice the amount of disk space is needed. Fallback is an optional feature; it can be turned on or off, based on the business need. When space is available, Fallback should be considered, due to its data-safekeeping ability.

Fallback Clusters

Fallback is a very powerful way to ensure data is duplicated and ready-to-go in the event of an AMP failure. However, when working with large Teradata systems, it is likely that there are numerous tables spread out across many AMPs. The more AMPs the system has, the greater potential for AMP failure. It is entirely possible to have multiple AMPs fail at the same time.

In order to mitigate the risk of data loss, as well as system downtime in the event of a multiple AMP failure, Fallback Clusters are used.

Fallback Clustering organizes groups of AMPs into clusters. Each cluster is responsible for maintaining all of the rows for its base table and Fallback data within the cluster.

Figure 6.3 illustrates clustering on an 8 AMP system. As you can see, the base table rows and their corresponding Fallback rows are contained within the same cluster. If one AMP fails in a cluster, Fallback can cover the missing AMP.

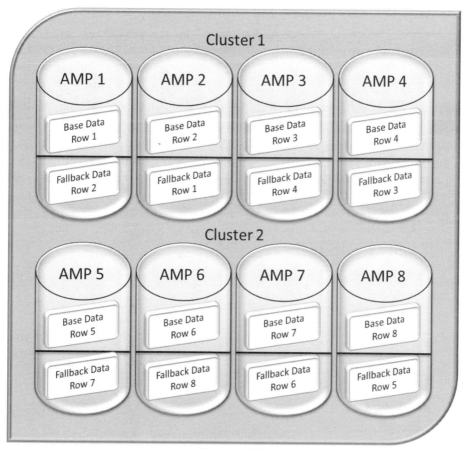

Figure 6.3

Down AMP Recovery Journal

The Down AMP Recovery Journal (DARJ) is used in the event of a down AMP. The journal begins immediately and is used to keep track of all changes that are made to the data while the AMP is down. The journal is kept on all of the remaining AMPs in the cluster, since the Fallback data for the down AMP resides on their disks. The DARJ is an automatic Teradata process, and cannot be modified or disabled.

The DARJ is very similar to the Transient Journal, in that it keeps a log of all data changes that should have been made on the original AMP. The DARJ is used to resynchronize the down AMP once it is back online. The DARJ is very useful because it prevents the need to completely rebuild the AMP's data from scratch when a failure occurs. Rather than rewriting all the data, only the missing transactions need to be applied. The DARJ uses available Perm space to keep its log. Once the AMP is restored and resynchronized, the DARJ is discarded and the Perm space is released. Figure 6.4 depicts a scenario where AMP 3 has failed:

OFFLINE

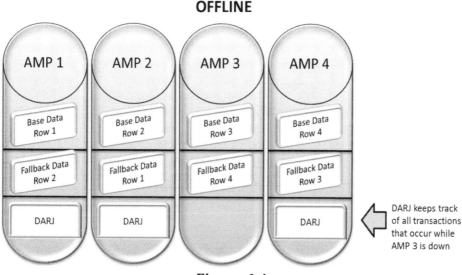

Figure 6.4

Redundant Array of Independent Disks (RAID)

Redundant Array of Independent Disks (RAID) is a technology that uses multiple disk drives to protect data from a single disk failure. All disks in a RAID configuration act as a single disk. The purpose of RAID is to ensure that, in the event of a drive failure, there is at least one more exact copy of the failed drive that is immediately available for use. In most cases, Teradata systems are pre-configured with RAID 1 as Figure 6.5 demonstrates.

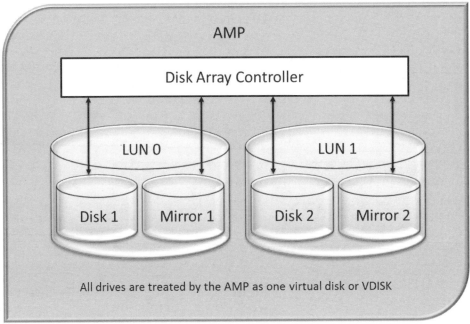

Figure 6.5

RAID 1 consists of two or more disks that are exact mirror images. When a mirror image fails, it does not impact the performance, space, or reliability of the remaining disk drives. Regardless of the number of mirror images, RAID 1 drives act as a single, virtual disk drive or VDISK. RAID 1 can require a significant amount of disk space, because an additional drive is required for every mirror image. A combination of RAID 1 and Fallback ensures that data is physically protected and fully redundant.

Cliques

Cliques are designed to protect Teradata in the event of a node failure. Basically Cliques are organized groups of nodes cabled to a set of disk arrays that work together to divide up a failed node's AMPs.

In a Teradata system, each AMP is connected to one, and only one, virtual disk. The virtual disk is actually a set of disks that operate as a single disk. Because the AMPs and their virtual disks are physically separate entities from the nodes, it is easy for Teradata to simply reassign the AMPs to another node within the Clique.

In Figure 6.6, we have a Clique with four nodes. If a node fails, Teradata will temporarily reassign the virtual disks from the down node to a backup node that is within the same Clique. In this case, all of the AMPs are migrated as evenly as possible across the remaining three nodes. The reassignment process is referred to as migration. Cliques are pre-configured by Teradata, based on your specific hardware configuration.

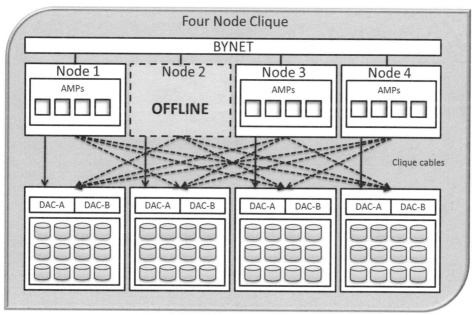

Figure 6.6

While the node is down, the AMPs can continue to perform read and write operations on the data contained on the virtual disks via the backup node. This will continue until the original node has been restored. Once restored, the AMPs return to their original node. Because a down node can result in a performance strain on the other nodes, Cliques work best on systems with multiple-node Clique configurations.

Hot Standby Node

A Hot Standby Node (HSN) is a backup node. It is a member of a clique, but it does not have AMPs configured, see Figure 6.7 for an illustration. When a node fails, the AMPs from the failed node migrate to the Hot Standby Node. Hot Standby Nodes are positioned as a performance continuity feature. Therefore, the performance degradation is 0%.

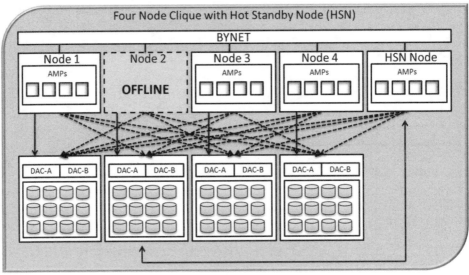

Figure 6.7

When the failed node is recovered, it becomes the new Hot Standby Node. Therefore, a second restart is not needed.

Hot Standby Nodes have the following characteristics:

- Is a member of a Clique.
- Typically do not participate in the Trusted Parallel Application (TPA).
- Can be utilized when a node fails in the clique.
- Provides a work around for unplanned outages.
- Are not required in order to bring a failed node back on-line.

Practice Questions

1) Which data protection mechanism provides true data mirroring onto another physical disk?
   A. Transient Journal
   B. Fallback
   C. Down AMP Recovery Journal
   D. RAID 1

2) Which of the three following are automatic data protection mechanisms of Teradata, and cannot be disabled:
   A. Transient Journal
   B. Fallback
   C. Down AMP Recovery Journal
   D. RAID 1

3) Which data protection mechanism keeps a log of all data changes belonging to a failed AMP, which are applied when the AMP is restored?
   A. Transient Journal
   B. Fallback
   C. Down AMP Recovery Journal
   D. RAID 1

4) Which statement is true of Fallback?
   A. The Fallback rows automatically migrate to a different clique when one AMP goes down
   B. The Fallback data is recorded twice, once in the primary Teradata system and once in the Fallback Teradata system
   C. The Fallback copy of a row is located on an AMP different from the AMP which holds the primary copy
   D. The Fallback copy of a row is always located on the same AMP which holds the primary copy

5) Which of the following are true about a Clique (choose three)?
   A. If a node fails, the virtual disks will be assigned to the remaining online nodes within the clique
   B. As long as the node is down, users cannot perform read and write operations
   C. The node migration is performed automatically by the Teradata system
   D. A node may be migrated to more than one backup node
   E. When the node is restored, AMPs migrate back to the original node

Chapter Notes

Utilize this space for notes, key points to remember, diagrams, areas of further study, etc.

_____

_____

_____

_____

_____

_____

_____

_____

_____

_____

_____

_____

_____

_____

_____

_____

_____

_____

_____

_____

_____

_____

Chapter 7: Security and Privacy

Certification Objectives

- ✓ Identify security mechanisms available to Teradata
- ✓ Identify privacy mechanisms available within Teradata

Before You Begin

You should be familiar with the following terms and concepts.

Terms	Key Concepts
Access Rights	LDAP, and user privileges / rights
View and Macros	Data access methods
Stored Procedures and UDF	Conditional and procedural functions
Roles and Profiles	Administer and manage access rights

Authentication

One method to control access to the Teradata Database is by utilizing LDAP. LDAP (Lightweight Directory Access Protocol) provides a means of managing and centralizing user accounts in a network environment. LDAP offers a scalable and secure approach to network management. By utilizing this method, you can use an LDAP to:

1. Authenticate users
2. Manage passwords
3. Provide a Single Sign-On strategy
4. Activate and deactivate accounts.

After users have been authenticated, then they are logged onto the Teradata Database. From there, they are authorized to access only those objects allowed by their database privileges.

Privileges and Access Rights

Your privileges and access rights define the types of activities you can perform on an object when you are logged onto the Teradata Database. The following operations require that you have specific privileges and rights as outlined in Figure 7.1:

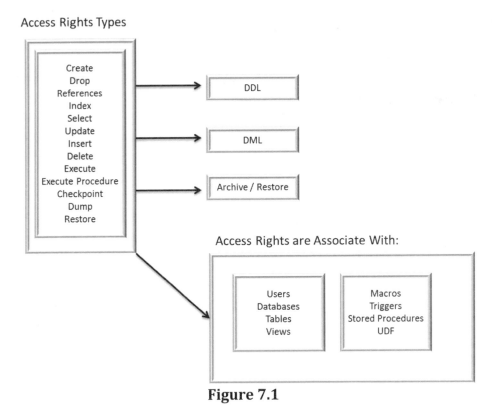

Figure 7.1

Teradata 12 Certification Study Guide

Privileges control user activities for manipulating database objects and data. This also includes the ability to grant access rights to other users in the database.

Access Rights Mechanisms

Access rights are categorized in one of three ways:

- Automatic (or Default) Access Rights - Automatic rights are privileges given to creators and, in the case of users and databases, their created objects. All rights are automatically removed for an object when it is dropped.

- Explicit Access Rights - Explicit rights are privileges conferred by using a GRANT statement. Explicit rights can be removed using the REVOKE statement.

- Implicit (or Ownership) Access Rights - Owners (Parents) have the implicit right to grant rights on any or all of their owned objects (Children), either to themselves or to any other user or database. Ownership rights cannot be taken away unless ownership is transferred.

In addition to access rights, Teradata database implementations are typically configured so users only access tables or applications via the semantic layer. This would include Views, Macros, Stored Procedures, and UDFs.

Views

A View is essentially a stored query that is accessible as a virtual table. Views, unlike tables, do not store data, but rather access data.

Therefore, Views are not physical entities and require no permanent space. However, they access actual table data using a SELECT statement. The SELECT statement is the main component of the view's definition, which is stored in the data dictionary. Underneath the covers, views fully leverage the massive parallel processing of Teradata. Views provide the following:

- Views can join together multiple tables to create a single virtual table. Views can help users to focus on getting the data they need, rather than spending substantial time writing SQL.

- Views can help to simplify data results. Many tables have complicated datasets that require aggregation and summarization before they are meaningful. Views are useful in performing these calculations behind the scenes.

- Views are useful because they can be written to exclude access to the sensitive columns, while providing access to the non-sensitive columns.

View Example

To create a view, you must specify a view name and the SQL statement. Views must be uniquely named, but only within their respective database/user.

In Figure 7.2, we create a simple view from our customer table. In this view, we are looking for all customers in area 2 whose policy amount is more than $500,000:

```
CREATE VIEW cust_area2_500plus_v AS
        SELECT cust_id
            , last_nm
            , first_nm
            , create_date
        FROM customer
        WHERE area = 2
            AND policy_amount > 500000;
```

Figure 7.2

Now that the view has been created, we can query the view. Suppose we want to further restrict the result set to only display customers who were created after the year 2008. Our new query looks like this:

```
SELECT * FROM cust_area2_500plus_v
WHERE create_date > '2008-12-31';
```

Figure 7.3

The results will now show all customers in area 2 with a policy amount greater than $500,000 and were created after 2008.

Macros

A Macro consists of one or more stored SQL statements, that when executed, are performed within a single transaction. Macros are often used to consolidate repetitive tasks and can also be used to perform complex operations. Macros, unlike tables, do not store data, but rather access data. Macros are therefore not physical entities and require no permanent space. Lastly, Macros reside in the data dictionary. Macros provide the following:

- Storing repetitive SQL statements and common routines saves time that would otherwise be spent re-writing the same SQL and helps reduce user SQL errors.

- Macros can be defined to receive input parameters from the user. The SQL statements can use the parameters as data values to allow for a parameterized query.

- Macros are also great for sharing. Macros are stored in the data dictionary database and can be accessed by as many users as necessary. Teradata has access rights which can be used to specify who can create, replace, drop, and execute the macro.

Macro Example

As discussed, macros are even more powerful when they are designed to accept input parameters. A user can specify the parameter(s) at execution time which are consumed by the macro. The input parameters are plugged into the macro's pre-defined variables in the macro syntax and then the macro executes the SQL command(s). Macros may have one or more parameters.

To execute a macro with parameters, they must be specified, after the macro name, within parenthesis. Each parameter must have a name and an associated data type. Within the macro syntax, the variables must be prefaced with a colon ":".

In Figure 7.4, we create a "policy amount increase" macro. This time, we specify the area number as a parameter, so we can give policy amount increases at the area level.

Teradata 12 Certification Study Guide

```
CREATE MACRO GlobalPolicyIncreaseByArea
(inArea INTEGER) AS

(UPDATE customer
  SET policy_amount = policy_amount * 1.1
  WHERE  area = :inArea;

SELECT * FROM customer; );
```

Figure 7.4

When executed, this macro will increase all customer policy amounts, within the specified area, by ten percent.

Macro Execution

To execute a macro, you must issue an EXECUTE statement, followed by the macro name and any required parameters as shown below.

```
EXEC GlobalPolicyIncreaseByArea (inArea=10);
```

Figure 7.5

All parameters must be enclosed within parenthesis, following the macro name. If no parameters are required, then parentheses are not required.

Stored Procedures

A Stored Procedure is a compiled set of SQL and procedural statements. Stored procedures are similar to programs. They must be compiled, they are procedural, and they can receive input and return output. Although stored procedures share some of the same functionality with macros, there are differences which are outlined below:

- Both Macros and Stored Procedures contain SQL and can receive input. However, stored procedures require physical storage.

- There are two types of stored procedures, internal and external. Typically stored procedures are internal, but Teradata allows for External Stored Procedures, which can be written in either Java™ or C++.

Stored procedures are also great for sharing because they are stored right on the database and can be accessed by as many users as necessary. Teradata has access rights which can be used to specify who can create, replace, drop, and execute the stored procedure.

Stored Procedure Example

Figure 7.6 is an example of a stored procedure. This procedure will delete the customer with the specified customer id from our Customer table:

```
CREATE PROCEDURE DeleteCustomer (IN inCust
INTEGER, OUT msg VARCHAR(20))

BEGIN

  DELETE FROM  customer
  WHERE cust_id = :inCust;
  SET msg = 'Delete Completed';

END;
```

Figure 7.6

Stored Procedure Execution

To execute a stored procedure, you must issue a CALL statement, followed by the stored procedure name and any required parameters.

In Figure 7.7, we execute our DeleteCustomer stored procedure. We pass in parameters of 100 and 200 (the two customer numbers) along with msg (which will return the message).

```
CALL DeleteCustomer(100, msg);
CALL DeleteCustomer(200, msg);
```

Figure 7.7

When executed, our stored procedure will return the message 'Delete Completed'.

User Defined Functions (UDFs)

A User Defined Function (UDF) is a compiled function, which can perform calculations and complete SQL commands, and are invoked as expressions from within SQL statements. UDFs are stored in their parent database/user's permanent space.

Teradata UDFs can be scalar functions that return single values, aggregate functions that return summary tables and table functions that return tables. UDFs are written in either the C or C++ programming language and must be compiled.

UDFs are very useful for performing calculations and summarizations of data. The ability to program in C or C++ allows for extended programming capability, beyond that of SQL. Examples of UDFs might include a function that checks if a value is numeric or a function that converts Fahrenheit into Celsius.

Roles

Roles can be viewed as a collection of access rights, which can be granted to individual users or groups in order to protect the security of data and objects within the Teradata Database. Any user granted a role can access all of the objects it has rights to. A database administrator can create different roles for different job functions and responsibilities, grant specific privileges on database objects to these roles, and then grant these roles to users.

Advantages of Roles

Advantages of roles include:

- Simplify access rights administration
- Reduce disk space usage

- Improved performance
- Less dictionary contention during DDL operations because the commands use less time.

A database administrator can grant rights on database objects to a role. These rights are then automatically applied to all users assigned to that role. When a user's function within his organization changes, it is easier to change his/her role than deleting old rights and granting new rights that go along with the new function.

Profiles

With profiles, a database administrator can define a set of system parameters. Assigning a profile to a group of users ensures that all group members operate with a common set of parameters as outlined below:

- Default database
- Spool space capacity
- Temporary space capacity
- Account strings
- Password security attributes

To manage this common set of parameters, a database administrator can create a different profile for each user group, based on system parameters that group members share or require.

Profiles provide two primary advantages:

- Simplify administration of parameters
- Easier control for user-level password security

Practice Questions

1) Which three mechanisms can be used to ensure security within the Teradata Database? (Choose three.)
   A. Access rights
   B. Spool limits
   C. Profiles
   D. Roles
   E. Views

2) Which one of the following types of Access Rights involves utilizing the GRANT command?
   A. Automatic
   B. Implicit
   C. Explicit
   D. System Owner

3) Which of the two following statements are true regarding views, as a security mechanism?
   A. A user must be granted access to the view in order to utilize
   B. Views are best for simple data results, and cannot be used to summarize data
   C. A user must have access to the base table in order to have access to the view
   D. Views can be used to exclude sensitive/private data columns from a user

4) What are three advantages of Roles?
   A. Easy control of user-level password security
   B. Improved performance
   C. Simplified Access Rights
   D. Reduced disk space usage
   E. Simplified administration of parameters

5) What are three parameters that can be configured within a Profile?
   A. Account strings
   B. Default password
   C. Spool and Temporary Space capacity
   D. Access Rights
   E. Default database

Chapter Notes

Utilize this space for notes, key points to remember, diagrams, areas of further study, etc.

Chapter 8: Teradata Tools and Utilities

Certification Objectives

- ✓ Identify the features and functions of data integration utilities
- ✓ Identify the features and functions of the management and access tools available within the Teradata product suite
- ✓ Identify the features and functions of the Teradata ARC utility
- ✓ Identify the tools in the Teradata Analyst Pack

Before You Begin

You should be familiar with the following terms and concepts.

Terms	Key Concepts
ETL Tools	Understanding BTEQ, FastExport, FastLoad, MultiLoad, and TPump
ARC	Backup and restoring options
Teradata Analyst Pack	Visual Explain, TSET. Index and Statistic Wizards

BTEQ

Basic Teradata Query (BTEQ) is a powerful and easy-to-use multipurpose utility that can be used in either a batch or interactive mode. BTEQ supports all types of SQL statements (INSERT / SELECT / DELETE / UPDATE), can create and utilize stored procedures, and execute certain Teradata commands. However, BTEQ is primarily used to do the following:

- **Data Loading** - BTEQ can load data directly from flat files. BTEQ can even read the output data directly from another

BTEQ job, using named pipes, without ever landing the data on a storage device.

- **Data Extraction** - BTEQ can create flat files from retrieved data (the output from a user's SELECT statement). BTEQ can also be used to provide the input data to another BTEQ job, using named pipes, without ever landing the data on a storage device.

- **Data Reporting** - BTEQ can create nicely formatted reports from retrieved data (the output from a user's SELECT statement). Data can be formatted and the reports can be designed with headers and footers.

FastLoad

FastLoad is a high performance data loading utility. FastLoad is the utility of choice when loading a large volume of data. FastLoad excels at reading flat files and can take input from any supported operating system platform. FastLoad can even read the output data directly from a FastExport job, using named pipes, without ever landing the data on a storage device.

FastLoad's speed advantage comes from its ability to leverage Teradata's parallel processing capabilities. Rather than loading in a row-by-row fashion, FastLoad loads data in 64K blocks in parallel per AMP.

However, FastLoad can only be used to load empty tables, and can only insert data; select/update/delete operations are not allowed, and can only operate on a single table. FastLoad is also a very system-intensive process, and only a limited number of FastLoad scripts can run on a Teradata system at a given time. Lastly, FastLoad is typically used to load an empty staging table that will be utilized to INSERT-SELECT into a populated table.

FastExport

FastExport is a high performance data extraction utility. FastExport is the utility of choice when extracting a large volume of data. FastExport excels at creating flat files but can also be used to provide the input data to a FastLoad job, using named pipes, without ever landing the data on a storage device.

FastExport retrieves the data specified from the user's SELECT statement, which is required in the FastExport script. FastExport can retrieve data from multiple tables, via the SELECT statement, and outputs the data into a flat file.

The speed advantage from FastExport comes from its ability to leverage Teradata's parallel processing capabilities. On each AMP, retrieved data is first stored in Spool Space and then sorted. Data is translated into 64K blocks, placed into the correct sequence, and returned to the client. FastExport's ability to return data in 64 blocks, as opposed to returning data in a row-by-row fashion, allows it to extract large amounts of data in a timely manner.

MultiLoad

MultiLoad is an extremely flexible and high-performance load utility that can be used for large volumes of data. Unlike FastLoad, MultiLoad can be used to update, upsert, or delete data from a table, as well as insert data. MultiLoad can work with up to five tables in the same job and each table can have up to twenty different inserts, updates, or deletes performed.

MultiLoad operates at the 64K block level. Data can be updated, inserted, upserted or even deleted. A minor drawback to MultiLoad is that the scripts are not as easy to create as a FastLoad or BTEQ script.

MultiLoad is very powerful and great care should be exercised when designing a script.

TPump

Teradata Parallel Data Pump (TPump) is a utility that is specifically designed to handle near real-time updates to Teradata. TPump can be used to insert, update, upsert, or delete data from a table. Like the other load utilities, TPump leverages Teradata's parallel processing architecture. TPump is most often used for small batches of updates, rather than large quantities.

TPump is a popular choice when on demand data processing is required because it has the ability to throttle data (the statement rate) to accommodate system throughput at peak and latent times. The statement rate can be changed within the TPump utility window and later decreased as users log on and for ad-hoc queries.

Teradata Parallel Transporter

Teradata Parallel Transporter (TPT) is unlike other utilities in that it operates as a multiple function load environment. TPT is a consolidated interface that leverages the Teradata parallel LOAD/UPDATE/EXPORT/STREAM operators, which utilizes FastLoad, MultiLoad, FastExport, and TPump underneath the covers. TPT focuses on the entire ETL process, rather than on just one subset. The concept behind TPT is to provide a user with the ability to perform an entire ETL task via a single unified job.

Because TPT utilizes the other utilities, the same rules and restrictions apply. The benefit from using TPT arises from its ability to consolidate an entire ETL process. This leads to easy maintenance, since many tasks are now contained in a single job. TPT also has an open API that allows 3rd party and in-house tools to communicate with Teradata.

Archive and Recovery

The Archive and Recovery (ARC, but often referred to as ARCMAIN) utility is used to backup and restore database and table objects, as well as to recover tables. ARC scripts can either be executed manually at the command line, or implemented with network attached tools. ARC allows for the following operations:

- Archive - ARC allows the archiving of data to physical storage, such as a tape device for an entire database or individual tables. Archiving can be utilized in two ways:

  - Channel-Attached (mainframe) - ARC is used to back up and restore data with Job Control Language (JCL) commands. ARC will backup data directly into the mainframe-attached tape subsystem.

  - Network-Attached - Third-party tape management products utilize ARC to back up data.

- Restore - ARC can restore an entire database or individual table(s) from a backup. Restore is most importantly used in the event of a system failure, such as an AMP failure. There are several scenarios where restoring objects from a backup may be necessary:

  - Non-Fallback tables after a disk failure.
  - Tables that have been corrupted.
  - Tables, views, or macros that have been accidentally dropped.
  - Problems resulting in damaged or lost database objects.
  - Archive a single partition.

- Copy - Similar to a restore, but the copy does not have to be placed onto the same system where the data originated. The copy operation is often used to create copies of a table and/or database onto another system.

- Recovery - For tables that are utilizing the journal options, recovery allows for the rollback and rollforward of data. Journals can be check pointed with a synchronization point and selected journal portions can be deleted.

Teradata Analyst Pack

Teradata Analyst Pack is a suite of tools consisting of the following:

- Teradata Visual Explain
- Teradata System Emulation Tool (TSET)
- Index Wizard
- Statistics Wizard

Below is an overview of the features and functions of each tool.

Teradata Visual Explain

Teradata Visual Explain provides the ability to capture and present the steps of a plan through a graphical user interface (GUI). This tool can provide improved insight and understanding of the Teradata Database Optimizer plan for a given SQL statement. Visual Explain also has the capability to perform comparisons of two or more SQL plans.

In order to provide a query plan, the Teradata Visual Explain tool retrieves the following:

- Database object definitions

- Data demographics
- Cost and cardinality estimates

The information gathered above can assists users in identifying the performance implications such as data skew, stale, or missing statistics.

Lastly, Visual Explain uses the Query Capture Database (QCD) to store query plans. This data can also be used by other Teradata Analyst Pack tools.

Teradata System Emulation Tool (TSET)

Teradata System Emulation Tool (TSET) provides the ability to emulate a production system by gathering all the necessary information in order to simulate the Optimizer process on another Teradata system (i.e. test). This information is used to generate query plans as well as simulate potential Optimizer related issues on a non-production system.

TSET also captures the following:

- System cost parameters
- Object definitions
- Random AMP samples
- Statistics
- Query execution plans
- Demographics

This tool also retrieves information by database, query, or workload. However, it does not export user data.

Index Wizard

Teradata Index Wizard is a graphical user interface (GUI) tool that provides an automated process for improving performance through the use of indexes on a particular workload. This tool guides the user through a step-by-step process by analyzing a database workload, and then offering suggestions for improving query performance. In addition, Index Wizard now has support for Partitioned Primary Indexes (PPI) along with offering recommendations for secondary indexes within a workload.

Statistics Wizard

Teradata Statistics Wizard is a graphical user tool (GUI), which enables users to analyze and automate the collection and re-collection of statistics. The end result of this process is better query plans and performance. Statistics Wizard is primarily utilized for the following:

- Provide recommendations to improve the query performance on a particular workload.
- Enables users to collect, or re-collect statistics on tables, indexes, or columns.
- Schedule the COLLECT STATISTICS activity.

In addition, Statistics Wizard can identify changes and provide recommendations on which tables should have statistics collected. This is based on the following:

- Data and table growth
- Columns and Indexes that would benefit from having statistics collected
- Recommend statistics for a specific workload

This tool also offers users the ability to accept or reject these recommendations.

Practice Questions

1) Which one of the following load utilities is best used for selecting data and returning formatted reports?
   A. BTEQ
   B. FastLoad
   C. FastExport
   D. MultiLoad
   E. TPump

2) Which one of the following is NOT true about FastLoad?
   A. Loads data in 64K blocks
   B. Only loads data into empty tables
   C. Can be used to load multiple tables, at once
   D. Can only be used to INSERT data, cannot UPDATE or DELETE data

3) Which three of the following describe how MultiLoad operates?
   A. Loads data in 64K blocks
   B. Can load up to five tables, in the same job
   C. Can UPDATE, INSERT, and DELETE data
   D. Can be used to handle near real-time processing, using small batches of updates

4) When should TPump be utilized (choose two)?
   A. When loading large quantities of data
   B. When you want to load data in 64K blocks
   C. When small batches of data must be loaded in near-real time
   D. When you need to throttle data to accommodate system peak times

5) Which of the following four load utilities does TPT leverage?
   A. BTEQ
   B. FastLoad
   C. FastExport
   D. MultiLoad
   E. TPump

6) Which one of the following ARC utility functions would be used in the event of an AMP failure?
   A. Copy
   B. Restore
   C. Archive
   D. Recovery

7) Which of the following Teradata Analyst Pack tools captures information on system cost, demographics, and AMP samples?
   A. Index Wizard
   B. Teradata Visual Explain
   C. Statistics Wizard
   D. Teradata System Emulation Tool

8) Which of the following Teradata Analyst Pack depicts a query plan and provide query cost estimates (choose one)?
   A. Teradata System Emulation Tool
   B. Index Wizard
   C. Teradata Visual Explain
   D. Statistics Wizard

Chapter Notes

Utilize this space for notes, key points to remember, diagrams, areas of further study, etc.

Teradata 12 Certification Study Guide

Chapter 9: Workload Management

Certification Objectives

- ✓ Describe the characteristics of workload types that Teradata supports
- ✓ List the purposes of workload management
- ✓ Identify the Teradata tools available to analyze and manage workload

Before You Begin

You should be familiar with the following terms and concepts.

Terms	Key Concepts
Workload Management Tools	Teradata Manager, TDWM, and Priority Scheduler
Workload Analysis	DBQL, Teradata Analyzer, and Performance Monitoring
TASM	Creating, managing, and designing workload definitions

Tools

Teradata Manager

Teradata Manager is a performance monitoring tool that simplifies the tasks of monitoring, controlling, and administering a Teradata system from a single interface. Basically, Teradata Manager collects, analyzes, and displays performance and database utilization information in either report or graphic format. Additional features of Teradata Manager are as follows:

- Graphical user interface (GUI) that makes the tools easy to use.

- It can monitor the Teradata Database for status, system utilization, and performance along with manage users / sessions.

- Provide information with graphs and reports that are easy to read and do analysis.

- Allows you to analyze the historical workloads.

Figure 9.1 shows the Teradata Manager main window along with all the menu options available to access, capture, configure, and analyze database information.

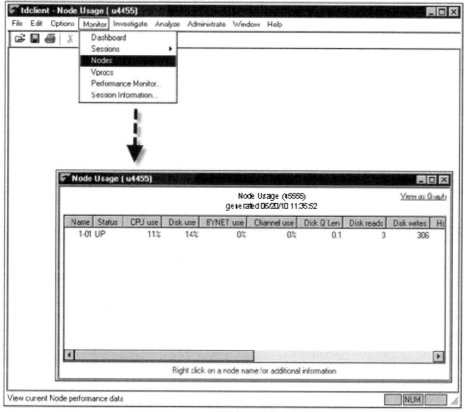

Figure 9.1

Teradata manager can also be customized and configured to fit specific needs of individuals or groups within your organization along with work on more than one Teradata Database simultaneously.

Lastly, Teradata Manager can also be configured as a client/server, which replicates performance data on the server that can be accessed by any number of clients.

Teradata Dynamic Workload Manager (TDWM)

Teradata Dynamic Workload Manager (TDWM) is a graphical user interface (GUI) tool that allows you to create / modify workloads in order to define rules for managing database access, increase database efficiency, and enhance workload capacity. As illustrated in Figure 9.2, TDWM can be configured to do the following:

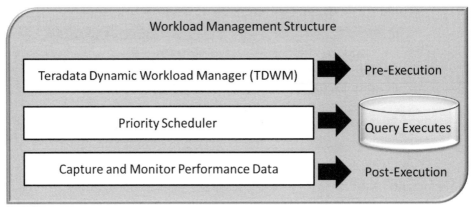

Figure 9.2

1. Pre-execution

   • Provide application resource control - what and how much - is allowed prior to execution

2. Priority Scheduler

   • Resource and Query Management
   • Manage and control the level of resources allocated based on different priorities of queries executing work
   • Assigns resources to users

3. Capture and Monitor Performance Data

- Enables DBA's or power users to examine the active workload
- Access historical data via Database Query Log
- Analyze query performance and behavior after completion

In addition, TDWM can be configured to run, suspend, schedule, or reject queries based on current workload and thresholds when submitted to the Teradata Database such as:

- Analysis control thresholds - Restrict requests that exceed a processing time, or result sets that exceed a defined rows size threshold.

- Object control thresholds – Define a workload definition that limits access to utilize database objects based on user IDs, tables, views, date, time, macros, databases, and groups.

- Environmental factors -Manage workload requests based on dynamic factors such as CPU, disk utilization, network activity, and concurrent users.

From a database administrator perspective, TDWM can be used to manage the following:

- Query Management - Query requests are intercepted, and are compared against criteria that are defined. If the requests fail to meet the criteria, or are restricted, they can be suspended, scheduled later, or rejected.

- Scheduled Requests - Enables clients to submit SQL requests that can be executed at scheduled off-peak times.

- Define Filters and Throttles such as:
    - Define Workloads
    - Operating periods Objectives

o Priority Scheduler facility (PSF) mapping/weights.

For example, User queries can be managed and scheduled to run during a specified time period. Results can be retrieved any time after the request has been submitted and executed by TDWM.

Note: TDWM is part of a new concept called Teradata Active System Management (TASM) which will be discussed later on in this chapter.

Priority Scheduler

Priority Scheduler is a resource management tool that controls the resource allocation (i.e. CPU) in a Teradata Database system. Priority Scheduler uses client based requirements and along with system parameters that determine the current activity level of the Teradata Database system. This functionality provides the following:

- Enables you to define a prioritized weighting system based on user logon characteristics.

- Balances the workload in your data warehouse based on this weighting system.

Database Query Log (DBQL)

The Database Query Log (DBQL) provides the ability to store historical records of queries such as duration, performance, query counts, and response times that can be charted and used for analysis. In addition, the SQL and processing steps can be compared in order to fine-tune queries for optimum performance. Lastly, DBQL can be customized to log information based on the user or query requests ranging from short transactions to longer-running analysis and data mining.

The Teradata Administrator Tool provides a GUI to configure Query Logging as shown in Figure 9.3:

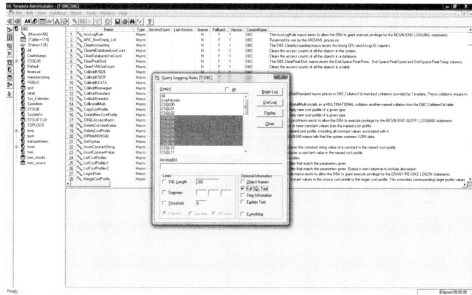

Figure 9.3

To access this interface, from Teradata Administrator, got to Tools > Query Logging

Teradata Workload Analyzer

Teradata Workload Analyzer utilizes DBQL data and current Priority Scheduler settings to analyze and identify classes of queries. From there, it can recommend workload strategies as outlined below:

- Offer workload allocation group recommendations and Priority Scheduler Facility (PSF) weight settings.

- Convert Priority Schedule Definitions (PD Sets) into new workloads.

- Recommend appropriate workload Service Level Goals (SLGs) and candidate workloads for analysis.

- Provide workload definitions directly from query history.

- Can be utilized to analyze, measure, and understand existing workload strategies and modify where necessary.

Note: Teradata Workload Analyzer can also apply best practices to workload definitions based on recommendations from Service Level Goal (SLG) objectives and priority scheduler settings.

Performance Monitor

The Performance Monitor (formerly called PMON) application can be started via Teradata Manager or used as a stand-alone application. Teradata Performance Monitor utilizes the Teradata Database PM / API to collect the following:

- Near real-time system configuration
- Resource usage
- Session information

This information can be gathered directly from the Teradata Database, through the Teradata Manager Server, or PC workstation. Figure 9.4 shows the Performance Monitor tool.

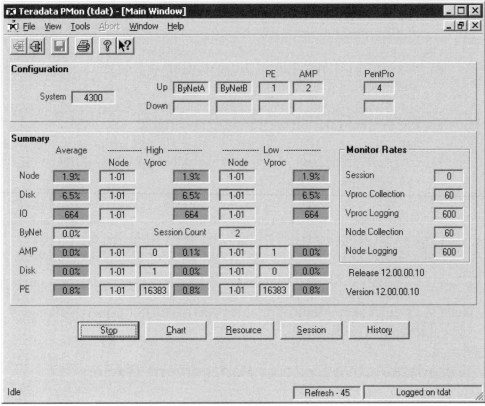

Figure 9.4

Teradata Performance Monitor displays information and performance data on four sets of screens, one for each of the following types of data:

- **General Health information (Configuration and Summary)** - This data is displayed on the main screen and is refreshed automatically at a user- defined interval.

- **Resource information (Nodes and Vprocs)** - This data is collected and displayed only when requested by the user. Graphs showing a user selected data point for each Node (or

Vproc) may be displayed by double clicking the required data point.

- **Session and Workload Information** - This data is collected and displayed only when requested by the user. The session summary screen shows all the sessions currently logged onto the system and allows the user to filter these sessions and to sort them in various ways. It also shows which sessions are currently blocked. Performance Monitor also allows you to examine the active workload(s).

- **Historical session information** - A list of historical session files is displayed. By choosing from this list the user may analyze a problem after the fact. The data itself is displayed on the regular Session Information screens.

Lastly, Performance Monitor enables you to ABORT sessions that are causing system problems.

Teradata Active Systems Management (TASM)

Teradata Active System Management (TASM) is made up of several products/tools that assist the DBA or application developer in defining and refining the rules that control the allocation of resources to workloads running on a system. These rules include filters, throttles, and "workload definitions". TASM is an enhanced compilation of three core products consisting of the following:

- Teradata Dynamic Workload Manager (TDWM) – Manages and monitors workload strategies
- Teradata Manager - Analyzes historical workloads
- Teradata Workload Analyzer (TWA) – Analyzes and recommends candidate workloads

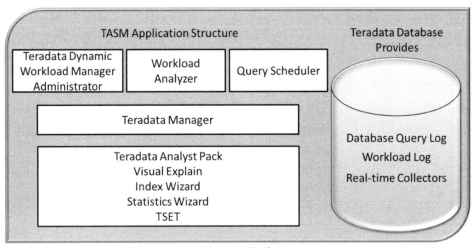

Figure 9.5

Teradata Active Systems Management (TASM), allows you to perform the following:

- Limit user concurrent access
- Monitor Service Level Goals (SLGs)
- Determine the workload on a system
- Prioritize and optimize mixed workloads
- Block or Reject user queries based on table access
- Provide consistent response times
- React to hardware failures

When utilized together, these tools can monitor workloads in real time along with providing historical reports based on resource utilization by workload. By analyzing this detailed information, workload definitions can be modified to improve query performance, and resource allocations.

Practice Questions

1) Which of the following tasks can be performed by Teradata Manager (choose one)?
   - A. Monitor system utilization
   - B. Define workloads
   - C. Assign priorities
   - D. Capture query history

2) Which three products are included within Teradata Active System Management (TASM)?
   - A. Teradata Workload Analyzer
   - B. Teradata Manager
   - C. Database Query Log
   - D. Teradata Dynamic Workload Manager

3) Which of the following items can be tracked by the Database Query Log (DBQL)?
   - A. Query duration
   - B. Query explain output
   - C. Query response times
   - D. Query error messages
   - E. All of the above

4) Which of the following tools can be used to view real-time resource usage and session information?
   - A. Teradata Workload Analyzer
   - B. Teradata Manager
   - C. Performance Monitor
   - D. Teradata Dynamic Workload Manager

5) Which of the following tools can be used to control the CPU usage allocation in a Teradata system?
   A. Priority Scheduler
   B. Teradata Manager
   C. Database Query Log
   D. Performance Monitor

Chapter Notes

Utilize this space for notes, key points to remember, diagrams, areas of further study, etc.

_____

_____

_____

_____

_____

_____

_____

_____

_____

_____

_____

_____

_____

_____

_____

_____

_____

_____

_____

_____

_____

_____

_____

Appendix

Answers to Chapter Practice Questions

Chapter 1	Chapter 2	Chapter 3	Chapter 4
1. ABD	1) BEDAC	1) AD	1) BD
2. ACD	2) A	2) BC	2) BCD
3. ACD	3) BC	3) D	3) ACD
4. AB	4) B	4) B	4) A
5. AB		5) A	5) D
		6) C	6) A

Chapter 5	Chapter 6	Chapter 7	Chapter 8
1) ADE	1) D	1) ADE	1) A
2) ACD	2) ACD	2) C	2) C
3) C	3) C	3) AD	3) ABC
4) ADE	4) C	4) BCD	4) CD
5) CD	5) ACE	5) ACE	5) BCDE
6) C			6) B
7) BDE			7) D
8) A			8) C
9) D			

Chapter 9
1) A
2) ABD
3) E
4) C
5) A

Index